Figures of the Salem Witch Trials

Figures of the Salem Witch Trials

Other books in the History Makers series:

America's Founders

Ancient Philosophers

Artists of the Renaissance

Astronauts

Awesome Athletes

Basketball Greats

Cartoonists

Civil War Generals of the
Confederacy

Civil War Generals of the Union

Cult Leaders

Dictators

Disease Detectives

Extreme Athletes

Fighters Against American Slavery

Fighters Against Censorship

Gangsters

Great Children's Authors

Great Composers

Great Conquerors

Great Male Comedians

Great Women Comedians

Gunfighters

Heroes of the Holocaust

Hitler's Henchmen

Home Run Kings

Influential Figures of
Ancient Greece

Influential First Ladies

The Kennedys

Lawmen of the Old West

Leaders of Black Civil Rights

Leaders of Women's Suffrage

Legendary Football
Quarterbacks

Magicians and Illusionists

Male Olympic Champions

Medieval Knights and Warriors

Native American Chiefs
and Warriors

Pioneers of the American West

Pioneers of the Internet

Pirates

Polar Explorers

Political Activists of
the 1960s

Presidential Assassins

Presidents and Scandals

Rock and Roll Legends

Rulers of Ancient Egypt

Rulers of the Middle Ages

Scientists of Ancient Greece

Serial Killers

Spies

Toymakers

Twentieth-Century American
Writers

Women Inventors

Women Leaders of Nations

Women of the American
Revolution

Women Olympic Champions

Women Pop Stars

History MAKERS

Figures of the Salem Witch Trials

By Stuart A. Kallen

LUCENT BOOKS
An imprint of Thomson Gale, a part of The Thomson Corporation

THOMSON
™
GALE

Detroit • New York • San Francisco • San Diego • New Haven, Conn.
Waterville, Maine • London • Munich

On cover: An elderly woman (*background*), her hands gesturing innocence, is led away by an officer of the law during the Salem witch trials. Insets show prominent figures of the trials (*clockwise from top right*): Cotton Mather, Tituba, and Samuel Sewall.

© 2005 Thomson Gale, a part of The Thomson Corporation.

Thomson and Star Logo are trademarks and Gale and Lucent Books are registered trademarks used herein under license.

For more information, contact
Lucent Books
27500 Drake Rd.
Farmington Hills, MI 48331-3535
Or you can visit our Internet site at http://www.gale.com

LIBRARY OF CONGRESS CATALOGING-IN-PUBLICATION DATA

Kallen, Stuart A., 1955–
  Figures of the Salem witch trials / by Stuart A. Kallen.
    p. cm. — (History makers)
  Includes bibliographical references and index.
  ISBN 1-59018-559-5 (hardcover : alk. paper)
  1. Trials (Witchcraft)—Massachusetts—Salem—History—17th century. 2. Witchcraft—Massachusetts—Salem—History—17th century. I. Title. II. Series.
  BF1576.K35 2004
  133.4'3'097445—dc22
                                                                          2004010686

Printed in the United States of America

Contents

FOREWORD

The literary form most often referred to as "multiple biography" was perfected in the first century A.D. by Plutarch, a perceptive and talented moralist and historian who hailed from the small town of Chaeronea in central Greece. His most famous work, *Parallel Lives*, consists of a long series of biographies of noteworthy ancient Greek and Roman statesmen and military leaders. Frequently, Plutarch compares a famous Greek to a famous Roman, pointing out similarities in personality and achievements. These expertly constructed and very readable tracts provided later historians and others, including playwrights like Shakespeare, with priceless information about prominent ancient personages and also inspired new generations of writers to tackle the multiple biography genre.

The Lucent History Makers series proudly carries on the venerable tradition handed down from Plutarch. Each volume in the series consists of a set of five to eight biographies of important and influential historical figures who were linked together by a common factor. In *Rulers of Ancient Rome*, for example, all the figures were generals, consuls, or emperors of either the Roman Republic or Empire; while the subjects of *Fighters Against American Slavery*, though they lived in different places and times, all shared the same goal, namely, the eradication of human servitude. Mindful that politicians and military leaders are not (and never have been) the only people who shape the course of history, the editors of the series have also included representatives from a wide range of endeavors, including scientists, artists, writers, philosophers, religious leaders, and sports figures.

Each book is intended to give a range of figures—some well known, others less known; some who made a great impact on history, others who made only a small impact. For instance, by making Columbus's initial voyage possible, Spain's Queen Isabella I, featured in *Women Leaders of Nations*, helped to open up the New World to exploration and exploitation by the European powers. Inarguably, therefore, she made a major contribution to a series of events that had momentous consequences for the entire world. By contrast, Catherine II, the eighteenth-century Russian queen, and Golda Meir, the modern Israeli prime minister, did not play roles of global impact; however, their policies and actions significantly influenced the historical development of both their own countries and their regional neighbors. Regardless of their relative importance in the greater historical scheme, all of the figures chronicled in the History Makers series made contributions to posterity; and their public achievements, as well as what is known about their private lives, are presented and evaluated in light of the most recent scholarship.

In addition, each volume in the series is documented and substantiated by a wide array of primary and secondary source quotations. The primary source quotes enliven the text by presenting eyewitness views of the times and culture in which each history maker lived, while the secondary source quotes, taken from the works of respected modern scholars, offer expert elaboration and/ or critical commentary. Each quote is footnoted, demonstrating to the reader exactly where biographers find their information. The footnotes also provide the reader with the means of conducting additional research. Finally, to further guide and illuminate readers, each volume in the series features photographs, two bibliographies, and a comprehensive index.

The History Makers series provides both students engaged in research and more casual readers with informative, enlightening, and entertaining overviews of individuals from a variety of circumstances, professions, and backgrounds. No doubt all of them, whether loved or hated, benevolent or cruel, constructive or destructive, will remain endlessly fascinating to each new generation seeking to identify the forces that shaped their world.

Hanging the Witches

Between January and September 1692 Salem Village in present-day Massachusetts was filled with superstition and fear of witches and the devil. During those few months thirteen women and six men were accused of witchcraft, carted to Gallows Hill, and hung by the neck until dead. Another man who was eighty years old was pressed to death under tons of heavy stones when he refused to cooperate with church authorities who charged him with being a wizard. Hundreds of other innocents were accused of witchcraft and dozens of them were imprisoned for extended periods of time without trial. At least four died in prison. Then, as quickly as the hysteria began, it ended.

It remains largely unclear to historians why such a miscarriage of justice took place in Salem and why it spiraled into a spree of executions. But an examination of the way people lived in seventeenth-century New England may help shed some light on this strange chapter in American history.

The Puritan Life

The people of Salem were Puritans, also called Congregationalists. In the seventeenth century the Puritans migrated to New England. They encouraged direct personal religious experience, stringent moral conduct, and simple worship services.

The strict Puritan theology included the absolute sovereignty of God and the total sinfulness of humans. Those who violated the strict rules of Puritan society faced severe punishments that were meant to humiliate as well as cause pain. Offenders might be locked in wooden stocks as townspeople threw rotten eggs at them. They were made to stand in public markets with notes stuck on their foreheads describing their offenses. And they were publicly whipped. While these penalties were doled out to those who spoke against the church, did not attend Sunday services, or even dared to kiss in public, the most severe punishments were meted out to those who were convicted of conspiring with the devil.

In such cases the church required no less than execution. Harsh rules of conduct applied to Puritan children as well as adults. There was little play or amusement, few toys or dolls. Childhood ended at an early age. By the time they were six or seven children were expected to work at all household chores. One Boston clergyman wrote in his diary that he expected his five- and six-year-old daughters to help upholster chairs and make curtains.

The only books in Puritan households were religious in theme. Some included graphic accounts by clergymen of supernatural incidents involving witches, spirits, demons, and Satan. They were sensationalized and meant to counter skepticism and disbelief at such occurrences. Few children read anything but the Bible, catechism (instruction on religious beliefs), a hymnbook, or the almanac.

Most girls did not know how to read because there were few schools for females in seventeenth-century New England. Young women of that time had little to feed their imaginations. There were no fairy tales or stories, no art, theater, or classical music. Boys were allowed to enjoy hunting, trapping, fishing, carpentry, and crafts, but girls were not allowed to participate in such activities.

"God Will Pour Out His Wrath"

Even the youngest children were forced to repress feelings of joy, rebelliousness, and anger. To exhibit anything but submissive behavior was to risk being branded as evil. Small children were told that they were

An offender is locked in a pillory in public view, one of several ways the Puritans of New England punished violators of the strict rules of their society.

in danger of spending an eternity in hellfire. Thoughtful children agonized over every move, fearful that they might sin by accident. Their terrors were not eased by the leading Boston minister, Cotton Mather, who, in the preface of a children's book, wrote:

> Do you dare to run up and down upon the Lord's day! Or do you keep in to read your [Bible]! They which lie, must go to their father the devil, into everlasting burning; they which never pray, God will pour out his wrath upon them; and when they beg and pray in hell fire, God will not forgive them, but there [they] must lie forever. Are you willing to go to hell to be burnt with the devil and his angels? . . . Oh, hell is a terrible place, that's worse a thousand times than whipping.[1]

Given the constant thundering by Puritans about Satan, sin, and witches' spells, it is not surprising that a sensitive child might be subject to fits and weeping and hysterical talk about witchcraft. And this is exactly what happened in late 1691 in the household of Reverend Samuel Parris where he resided with his wife, three children, his niece, a Caribbean Indian slave couple from Barbados named Tituba and John Indian, and an unnamed thirteen-year-old African slave.

In this seventeenth-century illustration, a sorcerer surrenders his Bible to Satan in exchange for a book of black magic.

A young Puritan woman reads the Bible as she spins wool. Puritan youth studied the Bible and prayed regularly to avoid an eternity in hell.

Fits and Convulsions

Among the children in the Parris family was a nine-year-old girl named Elizabeth, called Betty, who was steeped in her father's rigid beliefs. Elizabeth's best friend was her eleven-year-old cousin Abigail Williams. In early 1692 the girls began to display symptoms of hysteria, including fits and convulsions that occurred off and on for months.

Before long these symptoms spread to about eight other girls in the community, and Salem villagers feared a plague of witchcraft had come to their town. People from all over the countryside traveled to the parsonage to see the afflicted girls who began to have their fits on street corners. On one Sunday the tormented girls even had outbursts in church.

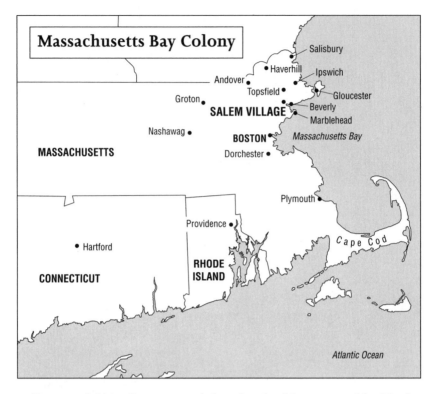

Massachusetts Bay Colony

Salisbury
Haverhill
Andover
Ipswich
Topsfield
Groton
Gloucester
SALEM VILLAGE
Beverly
Nashawag
Marblehead
MASSACHUSETTS
BOSTON
Massachusetts Bay
Dorchester
Plymouth
Providence
Cape Cod
Hartford
RHODE ISLAND
CONNECTICUT
Atlantic Ocean

Betty and Abigail announced that they had been cursed by Tituba and two other women, Sarah Good and Sarah Osborn (sometimes spelled Osburn). When their names were announced by the afflicted girls, four men of Salem appeared before magistrates (local members of the judiciary) and swore out arrest warrants for the women on suspicion of witchcraft.

When the accused were examined by town authorities on March 1, 1692, Tituba shocked the village when she claimed that she was indeed a witch. She also implicated Good, Osborn, and several other women. While these charges were serious, Tituba hinted that there were other witches yet undiscovered and her testimony set loose an unprecedented wave of paranoia in the tiny community. Villagers began to cast suspicious glances at their neighbors, wondering if they might be witches or wizards. Meanwhile, Good, Tituba, and Osborn were sent to a Boston jail. Osborn, already in ill health, was to die there on May 10, 1692.

Basking in the attention of the entire town, Abigail Williams and Betty Parris continued with their bizarre behavior after the women were sent away. Soon the circle of accused witches widened to snare more of Salem's rich and poor, sinners and saints, women and men. The local jails began to fill with accused witches—including a four-year-old girl who was the daughter of Sarah Good. To deal with the hundreds of allegations, Governor William Phips created a special court of oyer and terminer to hear the witchcraft cases. (The term "oyer and terminer" was used for English courts that were directed to hear and determine cases brought before judges.) Five judges, including three close friends of Cotton Mather, were appointed to the court. By modern standards, the trials that followed were outrageous. The accused had no legal representation and much of the testimony was hearsay, gossip, and unscientific assertions of devilry, witchcraft, ghosts, and other supernatural phenomena.

On June 10 Bridget Bishop became the first woman to swing from the hangman's rope. On July 19 five others, including Good, were hanged. On September 22 the last wave of executions commenced. Among the condemned was Salem's former minister George Burroughs. By this time, however, there were growing doubts that some of the town's most eminent citizens could be guilty of witchcraft. As fall turned to winter, the hysteria subsided. In May 1693 Phips pardoned more than fifty-two accused witches who were in prison or awaiting trial.

By the time it was over, as many as two hundred people had been arrested and accused. At least twenty-four died, and two dogs were also executed after being charged as witches' accomplices. In the following years Judge Samuel Sewall was the only one of the authorities who apologized for the miscarriage of justice that ended the lives of twenty-four people. Betty Parris and Abigail Williams escaped unscathed.

In 1711 the Massachusetts legislature passed a bill exonerating all of the accused and awarding about six hundred dollars to the survivors. As the years passed, the dark episode in Salem history induced the citizens to change the name of their town to Danvers. Although the witch hunt lasted little more than nine months, it has remained one of the most famous examples in American history of a population gone seemingly mad.

CHAPTER 1

Tituba

The witchcraft hysteria that overtook Salem in the early 1690s was fomented among a homogeneous population of white Puritans. Nearly all of these people were either born in England or could trace their roots directly back to the British Isles. However, Tituba, the woman at the center of the witch controversy, was an Arawak Indian. As Charles W. Upham wrote in *Salem Witchcraft* in 1867, Tituba "was spoken of as having come from . . . the Spanish West Indies, and the adjacent mainlands of Central and South America." [2]

Although Tituba faced serious charges, she was able to manipulate her accusers, telling them what they wanted to hear in order to protect herself from prosecution as a witch. And in doing so, she created a panic that resulted in hundreds of innocent people being charged with the capital crime of witchcraft.

Kidnapped into Slavery

Many aspects of Tituba's life are a matter of speculation, but as a slave, her days were likely filled with fear, pain, and tragedy. While the exact date of her birth is unknown, she is believed to have been between twenty-five and thirty when the witch panic gripped Salem. This would mean that she was born sometime in the 1660s. During that period the English ran a small slave trade between present-day Guyana in northern South America and the Caribbean island of Barbados. To obtain slaves, ship captains would sail up the Orinoco River into the South American rain forest. In order to capture the natives, the English often enticed Arawak to board their ships with the promise of friendly trade. When the Indians tried to leave, the British drew their muskets and ordered them to stay. The captives were put in chains, taken below decks, and transported to the Caribbean.

Some historians believe that a young Tituba and her mother could have been captured by Captain Peter Wroth in September 1674. According to Wroth's diary, at that time eight women and two children paddled their canoes up to the Englishman's ship, the *Sanoy*. After coming aboard to trade food and baskets, the women and children were grabbed by the sailors. They were then forcibly removed from the only land they ever knew and taken on a one-month journey to Barbados.

Whether or not Tituba was part of that horrifying experience, there is little doubt that when she arrived on Barbados, she was taken to the slave market in the English capital of Bridgetown. There, a few Indian captives mixed with hundreds of African slaves that were kept in pens similar to those that held farm animals.

Records show that young girls sold on Bridgetown wharves in the 1670s fetched between sixteen and eighteen pounds, equal to about five-hundred dollars today. It is thought that Tituba was purchased by planter Samuel Thompson. His ledger books, which have been preserved, show a slave named "Tattuba" among the girls under the age of fourteen on his plantation. Historians speculate this was a misspelling of "Tituba." Misspellings were common when the English attempted to translate Indian names.

Duties of an Indian Slave

Indian slaves like Tituba were generally treated differently from the Africans. While there were only several hundred Indians on the island, there were at least fifty thousand black slaves, most of whom toiled relentlessly in the sugarcane fields. The Indian slaves—especially

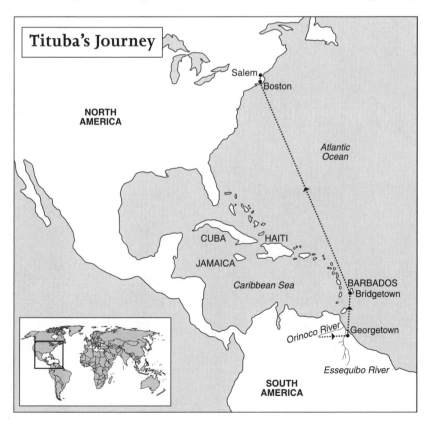

women—were used as domestic servants. As Elaine G. Breslaw writes in *Tituba: Reluctant Witch of Salem*, early explorers preferred Indians for household jobs:

> [The Arawak had] a reputation for being easygoing, less threatening than [other tribes], familiar with sedentary living patterns, and more amenable to European influence. . . . [To the] Barbados planters who wanted domestic servants, these gentle and generous people were a convenient source of labor. The Arawak women in particular were valued for their skill in preparing food, caring for domestic animals, and weaving cloth, in addition to cultivating root crops [such as sweet potatoes and cassava which was used to make tapioca].[3]

As a valuable domestic slave, Tituba would have been trained to cook, clean, and set the table in the manner of an English house ser-

During her early years as a slave, Tituba probably worked in a Barbados plantation house like this one.

vant. Unlike African slaves who generally wore only loincloths, Tituba would have been dressed as a proper seventeenth-century servant with a petticoat, smock, apron, cap, and shoes. In addition she would have been instructed in Anglican Christian beliefs, taught to speak English, and possibly to read. The personal possessions of a slave like Tituba were usually limited to a woven sleeping mat, a blanket, a cook pot, and cups and plates made from dried gourds. She would have lived in the slave quarters—small structures made from sticks and sugarcane stalks. Since these were largely built by Africans, they were said to resemble typical African villages. On the Thompson plantation, at least seventy-five African men, women, and children slaves lived in this manner.

Trances, Dreams, and Spirits

The Arawak were allowed to retain many of their traditional customs and beliefs because they were treated more favorably than the Africans. This included spiritual beliefs that would later strike fear into the people of Salem. Beliefs that Upham describes as "superstitions prevalent among [her] native tribes, materials which . . . heightened the [obsession] of the times, and inflamed still more the imaginations of the credulous [Puritans]."[4]

Like many indigenous cultures, the Arawak believed that the world was filled with spirits both good and bad. These spirits were found in trees, flowers, animals, the weather, water, and other elements of nature. Evil spirits were said to be ghosts of the dead that wandered the jungle at night causing bad luck, sickness, and death. The most frightening spirits, however, were not the dead, but living creatures called *kenaimas*. Like witches or devils, these creatures were human but could use supernatural powers to cause great suffering. The *kenaimas* could take on the shapes of monsters that were extremely hairy with protruding eyebrows. They could change shape at will, assuming the visage of any animal from a snake to a wolf. The *kenaimas* always came from outside the village to do their malevolent work.

The Arawak also believed that dreams were real. For example, if a person dreamed of *kenaimas*, it was not considered a nightmare but an actual brush with evil. On the other hand, good dreams were seen as positive forces in one's life.

The Arawak practiced many rituals in order to ward off evil spirits such as the *kenaimas*. Shamans went into deep trances so that their spirits could leave their bodies and fight evil spirits in their own world. Those who were not shamans rubbed red paint on their bodies to keep away sickness. They used small amounts of human blood in the same way in order to attract strength and courage. They also rubbed hot pepper juice into their own eyes causing temporary, painful blindness which was said to hide them from the sight of evil spirits. Breslaw describes how these beliefs colored the Salem witch hysteria decades later:

> Tituba's young world was informed by these beliefs, practices, and fears. She brought mental images of kenaimas, the value of trances, and the reality of dreams with her to Barbados from South America and did not lose them completely after her arrival in Massachusetts. Elements of these beliefs would surface later and with great consequence during her interrogation in Salem in 1692.[5]

From the Tropics to New England

Tituba's life on the Thompson plantation took a new direction in 1679, when Samuel Thompson fell ill. Sure that he was about to die, Thompson began to sell off his property and possessions, including his slaves. While the exact details are unknown, ownership of Tituba, who was between twelve and seventeen years old, was transferred to Samuel Parris. Tituba's new owner, however, was in Barbados only for a short time after he purchased her. By late 1680 Parris and Tituba were on their way to Boston.

One of the first things Tituba would have noticed as her ship approached Boston was the icy wind and frigid temperatures, unlike the tropical heat and humidity that had been her only experience up to that point. Upon landing, Tituba found a city quite unlike anything in Barbados. Boston was the largest and busiest city on the East Coast and was filled with brick buildings, warehouses, tidy streets, and shops.

The social climate was different as well. Between 1675 and 1676 a Native American rebellion in New England, called King Philip's War, resulted in the deaths of thousands of Puritans. Although the Native Americans lost the war, the white population of Massachusetts was suspicious and highly prejudicial against all Indians. The fact that Tituba was from South America was either not understood or mattered little to those who might have passed her on the street.

There was also intense religious prejudice toward Indian spirituality among the Puritans who followed a fundamentalist belief system much more rigid than the Anglican English of Barbados. Many New Englanders thought that Indians were witches in league with the devil and agreed with Puritan minister Cotton Mather, who described Indians as "Ravenous howling *Wolves* . . . horrid *Sorcerers*, and hellish *Conjurers*, and such as conversed with *Daemons*."[6]

With such attitudes, it is little wonder that a 1644 Massachusetts law required that Indians be converted to Christianity. As the head of the household, Parris was required to supervise Tituba as she prayed, read Bible verses, sang hymns, and practiced other elements of Puritanism. Like all other residents of Boston, Tituba was also required by law to spend all day Sunday in church.

During the rest of the week, Tituba was kept very busy with her domestic duties. By 1682 Parris had married Elizabeth Eldridge and the couple had two children; the second, a daughter named Elizabeth and called Betty. Samuel Parris was a successful businessman and soon obtained two more slaves, John Indian and another boy about thirteen, to help manage his growing household. Meanwhile, Parris began interviewing with the town fathers of Salem to fill the position

A woodcut depicts Boston Harbor as it looked when Samuel Parris and Tituba arrived in 1680.

of minister. By July 1689 the negotiations were complete. In November Parris, his family, and his slaves moved to the small village about fifteen miles north of Boston.

Moving to Salem

Tituba's new life in Salem would be quite different than what she had experienced in the relatively cosmopolitan atmosphere of Boston.

A Wampanoag warrior appears in full costume in this woodcut. A 1644 Massachusetts law dictated that all Indians be converted to Christianity.

Salem was a rural town that consisted of widely scattered farms surrounded by dense forest. Most of the inhabitants were poor, extremely religious, and lived a hard life, scraping a meager living from the soil. The official population was about 550 in about ninety households. Slaves, servants, and the homeless were uncounted, so the real number of residents was greater.

The six-member Parris family, which now included the couple's three children and his niece Abigail Williams, moved into the Salem parsonage along with the three slaves. This home that the church maintained for the parson had two rooms upstairs and two rooms downstairs. While the married couple slept in one room, and the children in another, Tituba and the other slaves slept on the kitchen floor at night.

Although the exact date is unknown, historians believe that Tituba and John Indian were married by 1689. Whether or not the couple ever had children remains unknown as there were no birth records kept for slaves. Some historians have suggested that Tituba had a child named Violet soon after she was married. Whatever the case, Tituba continued her regime of cooking, cleaning, and child care while Parris hired out John Indian to assist a local tavern keeper.

Trouble began in 1691, when Pastor Parris's preaching style fell out of favor with the townspeople of Salem. The village fathers stopped paying him regularly and in October voted to stop charging residents the usual taxes that paid his salary. As a bitterly cold winter approached, the Parris family had little income and no firewood that was supposed to be provided by the town. To make matters worse, a severe drought that year left food supplies low. In his Sunday sermons the pastor began to equate his political enemies with Satan. These sermons began to affect members of the Parris household. Tituba had a dream that an evil man disguised as a reputable clergyman was trying to coax her to hurt the village children. With a strong belief that dreams were, in fact, reality, this no doubt caused Tituba much stress.

The Devil Comes to Salem

Tituba was not the only member of the Parris household to experience stress over the pastor's uncertain job situation. Nine-year-old Betty began to experience unexplained illnesses accompanied by frightening hallucinations. Although the young girl was not allowed to play, Betty, her eleven-year-old cousin Abigail, and several other adolescent girls in Salem found ways to relieve their boredom. One was an innocent game by modern standards, in which the young girls tried to predict the occupations of their future husbands by pouring an egg white into a glass of water. The shape the egg takes, such as a hammer, or a paint brush, was believed to reflect the future husband's occupation.

This activity was anything but innocent for the Puritan girls in seventeenth-century New England, especially in this case. The egg white came up in the shape of a coffin. Soon Betty began to experience violent fits and convulsions. By February 1692 Abigail, twelve-year-old Ann Putnam, and Mercy Lewis, Elizabeth Hubbard, and Mary Walcott, all seventeen, joined the ranks of the "afflicted girls."

It is unknown whether Tituba knew of the egg-glass game, or was present when it happened. The fortune-telling game is part of an old English tradition, although similar methods of divination have been employed by indigenous cultures throughout the world. Whatever the case, the girls did not at first accuse Tituba as having participated in the episode.

Betty's and Abigail's inexplicable sufferings continued for weeks and became a matter of concern for the entire village. On February 25 a close neighbor, Mary Sibley, who lived up the road from the Parrises, decided to enlist Tituba to help find out who had placed the demonic curses upon the young girls. Sibley asked Tituba to prepare what was called a witch cake—rye flour mixed with the children's urine. It was baked in the ashes of a fire and fed to the family's dog. Sibley believed that the dog was a "familiar"—a messenger assigned to a witch by the devil—and the witch cake would help break the witch's spell that was afflicting the children. This form of "white magic" was viewed as sinister witchcraft by the Puritans. Tituba's willingness to help Sibley would soon come back to haunt the young woman from South America. As Breslaw writes: "The witchcake experiment brought the first public awareness that Tituba had knowledge of magical techniques. If such activities had been suspected before, no one thought to make reference to it in 1692."[7]

"The Devil Hath Been Raised Among Us"

Instead of helping, the witch cake incident only made matters worse. Parris condemned the preparation of the witch cake from the pulpit, thundering that Sibley and Tituba were "going to the Devil for help against the Devil."[8] He also said, "the Devil hath been raised among us, and his rage is vehement and terrible; and, when he shall be silenced, the Lord only knows."[9]

These invocations of Satan prompted Betty and Abigail to increase their bizarre behavior. The details of the hysterics were recorded by Salem's former parson Deodat Lawson in an essay with a long title typical of the day, *A Brief and True Narrative of Some*

A sketch depicts Tituba performing witchcraft in front of the Parris children. After several Salem girls fell ill, they claimed Tituba and other women were tormenting them.

Remarkable Passages Relating to Sundry Persons Afflicted by Witchcraft, at Salem Village Which Happened from the Nineteenth of March, to the Fifth of April, 1692. According to *A Brief and True Narrative,* Abigail Williams

> had a grievous fit; she was at first hurryed with Violence to and fro in the room . . . sometimes makeing as if she would fly, stretching up her arms as high as she could, and crying "Whish, Whish, Whish!" several times. . . . After that she run to the Fire, and begun to throw Fire Brands, about the house; and run against the Back, as if she would run up the Chimney, and, as they said, she had attempted to go into the Fire in other Fits. [10]

There were other symptoms as well. Both girls experienced temporary loss of sight and hearing; loss of memory, so that they could not recall what happened during the fits; a choking sensation in the throat; loss of appetite; and terrifying hallucinations.

On February 29 Abigail and Betty named their tormentors, pointing to Sarah Good and Sarah Osborn. They also dramatically implicated Tituba. According to the 1702 book *A Modest Inquiry into the Nature of Witchcraft* by John Hale:

> The Afflicted persons cryed out of the Indian Woman, named Tituba, that she did pinch, prick, and grievously torment them. ... These Children were bitten ... their arms, necks, and backs turned this way and that way, and returned back again, so as it was impossible for them to do themselves . . . their limbs wracked and tormented so as might move an heart of stone, to sympathize with them. [11]

When the children were examined by Dr. William Griggs, he pronounced, "The evil hand is upon them; the girls were victims of malefic witchcraft." [12]

"Kill the Children"

On the morning of March 1, 1692, practically everyone in Salem and the surrounding area crowded around Sam Ingersoll's tavern. They were waiting for the magistrates to arrive—and to get a glimpse of Tituba and the accused witches. Nothing this exciting had ever happened in the Salem area and farmers and housewives ignored their chores to gather in small groups to gossip about the accused. Many recalled strange incidents that had seemed unimportant at the time, but now appeared to incriminate the alleged witches.

By the time magistrates Jonathan Corwin and John Hathorne arrived the crowd had grown too large for the tavern, so the church meeting house was opened. It, too, quickly filled with spectators. Before long the preliminary examination got under way. The three accused women were questioned by the two Salem magistrates, and Tituba was last.

Tituba's court appearance was recorded in great detail by an educator named Ezekiel Cheever. In the testimony, Tituba seems to be incorporating her traditional beliefs with a previous dream she had about the evil man from Boston. Hathorne asked the frightened woman:

> "Why do you hurt these children?"
>
> "I do not hurt them."
>
> "Who is it then?"
>
> "The Devil, for aught I know."
>
> "Did you never see the Devil?"

A Modeſt Enquiry
Into the Nature of
Witchcraft,
AND
How Perſons Guilty of that Crime may be *Convicted* : And the means uſed for their Diſcovery Diſcuſſed, both *Negatively* and *Affirmatively.* according to *SCRIPTURE* and *EXPERIENCE.*

By John Hale,
Paſtor of the Church of Chriſt in *Beverley,*
Anno Domini 1 6 9 7.

When they ſay unto you, ſeek unto them that have Familiar Spirits and unto Wizzards, that peep, &c To the Law and to the Teſtimony ; if they ſpeak not according to this word, it is becauſe there is no light in them, Iſaiah VIII. 19, 20.
That which I ſee not teach thou me, Job 34 32.

BOSTON in N. E.
Printed by *B. Green,* and *J. Allen,* for *Benjamin Eliot* under the Town Houſe. 1702

The title page of John Hale's account of the Salem witch trials, A Modest Enquiry into the Nature of Witchcraft, *is shown here.*

27

"The Devil," said Tituba, "came to me and bid me serve him."

"Who have you seen?"

"Four women sometimes hurt the children."

"Who were they?"

"Goody [Sarah] Osburn and Sarah Good, and I do not know who the others were. Sarah Good and Osburn would have me hurt the children, but I would not."

[The court clerk wrote:] (She further saith there was a tall man of Boston that she did see. . . .)

"[There] is four women and one man, they hurt the children, and then they lay all upon me; and they tell me, if I will not hurt the children, they will hurt me."

"But did you not hurt them?"

"Yes; but I will hurt them no more."

A historian poses inside a re-creation of Salem's church meetinghouse, where Tituba and others accused of witchcraft were given pretrial hearings.

"What have you seen?"

"A man come to me, and say, 'Serve me.'"

"What service?"

"Hurt the children: and last night there was an appearance that said, 'Kill the children'; and, if I would not go on hurting the children, they would do worse to me."

"What is this appearance you see?"

"Sometimes it is like a hog, and sometimes like a great dog. . . ."

"What did it say to you?"

"The black dog said, 'Serve me'; but I said, 'I am afraid.' He said, if I did not, he would do worse to me."

"What did you say to it?"

"I will serve you no longer. Then he said he would hurt me; and then he looks like a man, and threatens to hurt me." [The court clerk writes] (She said that this man had a yellow-bird that kept with him.) "And he told me he had more pretty things that he would give me, if I would serve him."

"What were these pretty things?"

"He did not show me them."

"What else have you seen?"

"Two cats; a red cat, and a black cat."

"What did they say to you."

"They said, 'Serve me.'"

"When did you see them?"

"Last night; and they said, 'Serve me'; but I said I would not."

"What service?"

"She said, hurt the children." [13]

Tituba continued, saying that the specter had brought her to Elizabeth Hubbard that morning and that Tituba was made to pinch the girl. Then she was asked about tormenting the other afflicted girls. Tituba related that the evil ones ordered her to kill one girl with a knife. In order to get to the girl's house, she traveled like a witch. "We ride upon sticks, and are there presently." [14] Tituba also described some monstrous creatures that sounded like the *kenaimas* of her tribe. One creature looked like a woman but had wings. Another thing was hairy and walked upright like a man. When Tituba mentioned this,

Abigail Williams said she saw the same creature, and it turned into the shape of Osborn.

Tituba continued claiming the devil had shown her a book with nine red bloodlike marks—two made by Good and Osborn. Good had supposedly confessed to Tituba to making the marks but Osborn would not. Other marks, Tituba claimed, were made by women that she did not know.

As Tituba was speaking, the girls once again fell into fits. They claimed that Tituba had been pinching and pricking them during her entire testimony. When the magistrate asked Tituba who was afflicting the girls, the woman said she saw the shape of Sarah Good tormenting them.

During the final testimony, the courtroom became hushed as Tituba confessed to the crime of witchcraft. It is unclear why she did this, but it was known that very few people had ever been executed for witchcraft in America at that time. In addition, an admission of guilt meant she would not be executed. Instead she could be rehabilitated by prayer and counseling. Ironically, only those who professed their innocence to the end were hanged. Whatever her reasons, by the end of the examination Tituba herself began having seizures like those of the girls.

Freed from Prison

Tituba was questioned by authorities for five days. Rather than clearing the air, however, the testimony only served to frighten the community and reinforce the idea that diabolical evil was at work in their town. Her words also provided a legal basis to pursue other witches, as the judges felt it was their moral duty to hunt down every possible witch in town.

Tituba was carted off to a Boston jail on March 7, even as witch fever began to spread through Salem. By March 11 four adult women began to exhibit hysterical behavior similar to that of the afflicted girls. By the end of the month at least a dozen women and girls were afflicted, and charges and countercharges of witchcraft wreaked havoc on the social structure of the formerly peaceful village. During the next seven months, hysteria and fear ruled Salem as hundreds were arrested and twenty-four were executed. This was all a result of Tituba's testimony that nine villagers had made marks in the devil's book.

Meanwhile, Tituba remained in the Boston jail, abandoned by Parris. This jail would be described today as a torture chamber. The woman was kept in a dungeon that was dark and so damp that water ran down the walls. She was given only enough food or drink

During the final testimony, Tituba confessed to the crimes of witchcraft. Her confession provided a legal basis for charges against other Salem residents.

to keep her alive and there was little heat in the bitterly cold winter. Her arms and legs were weighted down or chained to walls ostensibly so her specter could not escape and wreak havoc.

Although Massachusetts governor William Phips put an end to the witch trials in October 1692 and ordered all prisoners released, the accused were not allowed their freedom until they had paid the jailers for their food and other expenses. They even had to pay the cost for making the manacles and iron chains that kept them bound to the walls twenty-four hours a day. Tituba, with no money of her own, languished in prison until April 1693 when an unnamed person paid the seven pounds she owed in jail fees. There are no further records of Tituba's life after this period, but it is assumed that the unfortunate woman became the property of the person who paid for her release.

Although Tituba disappeared, her testimony launched a frightening chapter in American history. Were it not for the young woman who was kidnapped in South America by an English slaver, few people would have cause to remember Salem as anything but a small town in seventeenth-century New England.

CHAPTER 2

Samuel Parris

As pastor of Salem Church during the height of the witch hunts, Samuel Parris is one of the most controversial figures involved in the episode. Not only was he responsible for bringing Tituba to town at a time when Indian slaves were regarded with contempt, but he has also been accused of fanning the flames of hysteria in order to cement his religious authority. As Larry Gragg writes in *A Quest for Security,* many historians have certified Parris "as one of America's more prominent scoundrels." [15]

Others have argued that Parris was simply a failed businessman who was desperately trying to please the people of Salem in order to keep his job as the town's pastor. As Paul Boyer and Stephen Nissenbaum write in *Salem Possessed: The Social Origins of Witchcraft,* Parris's life up to that point had been "marked by economic setbacks, career frustrations, and mounting anxiety about what the future might hold." [16] In short, the authors suggest that Samuel Parris was a frightened man living in terrifying times when death from disease, starvation, and Indian attacks were all too common in the colony.

Samuel Parris was born in London in 1653, a younger son to Thomas Parris, a cloth merchant whose family had land holdings in Ireland and Barbados. Samuel had an older brother named John. Little is known about Samuel's early life, but in the late 1660s his father moved to Barbados to oversee his plantation, a moderately successful operation that depended on slave labor to produce sugar.

During this time, Thomas Parris befriended John Oxenbridge, a Puritan minister who moved to Boston in 1670 to become pastor of that city's First Church. Some historians believe this friendship influenced Thomas to send Samuel to Harvard College in Cambridge in 1671. Tuition to Harvard was expensive, with a four-year degree costing as much as a small house in Boston. It was considered to be worth it, however, as a Harvard degree guaranteed its holder entry into the world of the English ruling classes in America.

In the 1670s Harvard was a Puritan college and run in the typically strict Congregationalist manner. Long hair was forbidden as were fancy clothes and gambling. The school day lasted from 6:00 A.M.

In 1671 Samuel Parris enrolled at Harvard University, then a strict Puritan college.

to 9:00 P.M. Students attended prayer meetings twice a day where they memorized Bible verses, listened to readings, and were quizzed on the sermons that they had heard in church on the previous Sunday. Classes consisted of morning lectures where Hebrew, Greek, logic, ethics, and divinity were studied, followed by afternoon discussions of those topics.

Parris never graduated from Harvard, leaving in 1673 when his father died. As Gragg explains, however, the young man benefited from his Harvard education nonetheless:

> The instructors enhanced his understanding of the reformed faith, and they provided models of the intellectual discipline and skill required to interpret scripture and function as a Puritan clergyman. . . . Moreover, in his undergraduate days, Parris made friends, men with whom he remained in contact. Many years later, for example, he [remained friends with] Stephen Sewall [brother to a judge at the Salem witch trials].[17]

The Barbados Estate

Thomas Parris was a wealthy man who, upon his death, left considerable land holdings to his sons. To the twenty-year-old Samuel,

Thomas deeded his entire estate on Barbados, which according to the will consisted of "one hundred and seventy acres or thereabouts together with all the christian servts slaves cattle sheep stock buildings mills copper stills utensils or other necessarys and appurtences standing growing lying or being thereon." [18] Although this was only a fraction of the inheritance received by Samuel's brother John, it was still a large holding, estimated to be worth seven thousand pounds. While comparisons to modern figures are difficult, this sum is estimated to equal several million dollars. This inheritance allowed Samuel to move to the Barbados capital of Bridgetown and live like a wealthy gentleman. (It is known that Samuel's mother was dead by this time, as Thomas left instructions that he wished to be buried next to her.)

Samuel left the day-to-day operation of the plantation to others, while he worked as a financial and sales agent for the islands' planters, arranging loans and sales of their crops. Parris's dreams of living the life of an aristocrat were shattered in August 1675 when a major hurricane hit Barbados, killing at least two hundred people, destroying one thousand homes, and ruining the sugarcane crop that was due to be harvested in a few weeks.

Historians believe that this three-hour storm wiped out all the crops and most of the buildings on Parris's plantation. In the years

A woman harvests sugarcane in Barbados. In 1675 a hurricane destroyed Samuel Parris's Barbados sugarcane fields.

that followed this setback, life on Barbados seemed to grow increasingly intolerable for Parris. Sugar prices reached all-time lows and tensions ran high between the white planters and the slaves, who outnumbered the owners by a ratio of two to one. Driven by a combination of fear and failing finances, Parris decided to sell his plantation and move to Boston. During his final months on the island, however, Parris purchased a slave—a female Arawak Indian named Tituba. She traveled with Parris from the tropical island to frigid New England in the winter months of 1680.

Father, Church Member, and Merchant

Although Boston was the largest city in the colonies, it contained only about seven thousand people when Parris arrived there. By 1681 Parris was in the mercantile business, trading American products such as lumber, corn, and rice for imported goods such as Caribbean sugar and English clothing, liquor, and furniture—items that were in great demand in the New World.

Parris wasted little time becoming a family man after moving to Boston. Apparently he was married to Elizabeth Eldridge almost immediately upon his arrival, because the couple had a son, Thomas, by October 1681. A year later a daughter Elizabeth, or Betty, was born, and at some point Parris's young niece Abigail Williams also moved in with the family.

Hoping to advance socially in his newly adopted city, Parris joined Boston's First Church. Through the church he applied for, and was granted, what was called freeman status. Freemen were the only colonists allowed to vote and participate in government. Membership was restricted to mature male church members who were said to have experienced a transforming spiritual experience as confirmed by church leaders. As a freeman, Parris began to participate in Boston government. By 1684 Parris was serving as foreman on the respected court known as the Jury of Attaints and Appeals. In a few short years, Parris was an accomplished Boston gentleman, as Gragg writes: "Husband, father, church member, and merchant, Samuel Parris had by age thirty achieved much, and the future appeared bright." [19]

It was common for Boston gentlemen to have their portraits painted, and during this period Parris commissioned a miniature painting of himself. His appearance is described by Peter Charles Hoffer in *The Devil's Disciples:* "In [the painting Parris] is dressed as a man of modest means, sober, a not quite handsome man, with a long face, full but tightly set lips, large eyes, and a straight, prominent nose. He appeared wary, almost weary, but the face was still unfinished—a man midway through life, seeking its meaning perhaps." [20]

Negotiating a Position

Parris might have looked wary because his bright future seemed to be dimming rapidly by the mid-1680s. He had been sued by a wealthy Boston merchant for failing to repay a large loan and was facing a lawsuit by another man. By 1686 Parris appears to have decided that he would never achieve success as a merchant and instead decided to become a clergyman. He began by preaching in nearby towns, filling in for absent ministers. When substitute jobs were not available, Parris spoke at church meetings and to private groups. Sometime after the birth of his third child, Susanna, in 1687, Parris was contacted by the town fathers of Salem. He was invited to lead the village church first in the spring of 1688 and again in the fall.

The isolated Salem was a town in turmoil. There had been several land disputes between neighbors in the village's short history, and the town's two leading families, the Putnams and the Porters, often feuded with one another. Oftentimes the battles centered on the direction the town's church should take, and the previous three ministers had fled under contentious circumstances before their contracts had expired. By the time Salem's church committee was making overtures to Parris, the town had not had a successful minister in twenty years.

Parris's arrival did little to soothe the souls of the quarrelsome townsfolk, however. Having survived for sixteen years as a hard-nosed businessman, Parris was quite demanding during discussions with the three-man committee that was formed to negotiate the terms of his contract. What resulted, according to Boyer and Nissenbaum, was "a full year of hard and divisive negotiations to which . . . he subjected the Village between its initial approach to him and his final decision to accept." [21]

The town was divided over Parris's demands, but he was backed by Captain John Putnam, patriarch of the powerful

Samuel Parris became minister of the Salem church in 1688.

Salem family. In April 1689 the church committee agreed to pay Parris twenty pounds annually in cash along with forty pounds worth of corn and other provisions. Parris also got them to agree to a detailed eight-point document that stated Parris's wages would increase if money became more plentiful, that firewood would be given freely, and financial contributions made to the church would be given directly to benefit the minister. In addition, Parris would be given the parsonage, a barn, and the surrounding meadow for his livestock.

"A More Primitive Way of Life"

The Parris family that moved into the Salem parsonage in September 1689 consisted of Samuel and his wife, their three children, Abigail Williams, and three slaves—Tituba, John Indian, and an unnamed thirteen-year-old. For a London-born, Harvard-educated man who had traveled extensively, the trip to rural Salem, according to Hoffer, was "back into a more primitive way of life, ruder, less accomplished, more suspicious of strangers."[22] It was also a world of wilderness where wolves, bears, and wildcats wandered the dark woods that were broken only here and there by small farmhouses.

The parsonage the Parrises inhabited was luxurious by Salem standards. It was about forty-two by twenty feet with two rooms upstairs and two downstairs. There was also an unfinished attic, a cellar beneath the building, and a lean-to used for storage along one outer wall. Elaine G. Breslaw describes the way the Parris family chose to utilize the rooms of the parsonage:

> On the ground floor, one of the two rooms was kept as a parlor that held the best bed for Elizabeth and Samuel Parris and the baby [Susanna]; a second bed in the corner provided a sleeping place for the other children, Thomas now eight and Betty seven. They might have been joined by Parris's niece Abigail Williams. The other downstairs room, the hall, contained a cupboard or chest, a table, and backless benches. Parris used it as a study to prepare his sermons and conduct Bible readings for his household. The hall also served as the kitchen where Tituba and John and the African boy probably spread pallets at night to sleep. The upstairs chambers were set aside for the storage of foodstuffs and out-of-season tools, but might also have served as a sleeping space for the slaves and servants in the family. . . . All rooms served a multiplicity of purposes and the living arrangements made no provision for personal privacy for anyone.[23]

As Salem's minister, Samuel Parris delivered two sermons every Sunday and a lecture on Thursdays at this Salem meetinghouse.

The Parrises must have been well settled into their new home when the ritual held to formally swear in the minister, the "Embodying of a Church in Salem Village," took place on November 18, 1689. Gragg describes the scene: "Undoubtedly the meetinghouse was packed for the day of prayer, fasting, ordination ritual, Samuel Parris's sermon, and ultimately the congregation's entry into a covenant." [24]

In the two years that followed, Parris preached two sermons every Sunday, one in the morning and one in the afternoon. Attendance at both services was considered mandatory, and each one lasted at least two hours. On Thursday evenings he delivered a lecture in which attendance was voluntary. As his congregation swelled, the tiny twenty-eight- by thirty-four-foot meetinghouse grew extremely crowded. Parris seemed to finally find success in his life.

Of all the sermons Parris wrote, more than fifty have survived. Most are typical of other Puritan preaching of the day. For example, Parris often reminded his congregation that humans were steeped in sin, saying: "Thou art in this life a rotten, putrid, vile, corrupt, & abominable thing in the eyes of God." [25] Perhaps more unusual, on one occasion

Parris closed one of his early sermons by reminding the townsfolk that he was God's emissary and, as such, he should be held in an exalted position, telling them:

> You are to pay me that Reverence which is due to an Embassadour of Christ Jesus. You are to bear me a great deal of love. . . . You are to obey me. . . . You are to pray for me and to pray such and fervently always for me, but especially when you hear from God by me. . . . You are to endeavor . . . to make my heavy work . . . light and cheerful . . . and not . . . to make life among you grievous, and my labor among you unprofitable. [26]

Trouble in the Parsonage

Despite his instructions to the people of Salem, the problems faced by previous pastors did not vanish when Parris took to the pulpit. As early as one month after his ordination, more than 20 percent of the taxes that were owed by villagers for the pastor's salary remained unpaid. In addition, the meetinghouse had fallen into disrepair, and the money to fix it, owed by congregation members, was not forthcoming. The land disputes continued between villagers, and a bitter disagreement arose concerning the land surrounding the parsonage that was supposed to be given to Parris. As early as 1689, as problems piled atop other problems, Parris began to castigate his congregation in ever-harsher terms, saying some were "as senseless as the seats they sit on, pillars they lean on, dead bodies they sometimes tread on." [27]

As Parris's battles with his congregation increased, fewer townsfolk were willing to pay their taxes to provide his salary. And as his financial difficulties grew more acute in early 1692, a new, much more serious threat came to the Parris household. In December 1691, unbeknownst to the pastor, Parris's nine-year-old daughter Betty and her eleven-year-old cousin Abigail played a game by which they tried to predict the future by pouring an egg white into a glass of water. The shape the egg would take was believed to determine the occupation of the girls' future husbands. According to Hale, the egg appeared as "a specter in the likeness of a coffin." [28] This frightened the girls so badly that by late January 1692, Betty began to experience violent fits, dashing about the house, diving off of furniture, and screaming uncontrollably. By February 1692 Abigail and several other girls in town were also afflicted with this behavior, believed to be demonic possession created by local witches.

Even as this was happening, Parris was preparing a lawsuit against the village of Salem to collect the wages that had been promised to him. This further divided the church into those who supported the pastor and those who were against him. That the troublesome and possibly demonic influences of the afflicted girls took place in the parsonage must have scandalized Parris's detractors. As Gragg writes, Salem villagers "expected their new minister to be beyond reproach

In 1689 the Puritan minister Cotton Mather published an account of demonic possession in New England. Three years later, Samuel Parris's daughter and other Salem girls claimed to be victims of possession.

MEMORABLE PROVIDENCES,

Relating to

WITCHCRAFTS

And POSSESSIONS.

A Faithful Account of many Wonderful and Surprising Things, that have befallen several Bewitched and Possessed Persons in New-England. Particularly, A NARRATIVE of the marvellous Trouble and Releef Experienced by a pious Family in Boston, very lately, and sadly molested with EVIL SPIRITS.

Whereunto is added,

A Discourse delivered unto a Congregation in Boston, on the Occasion of that Illustrious Providence. As also.

A Discourse delivered unto the same Congregation; on the occasion of an horrible Self-Murder Committed in the Town.

With an Appendix, in vindication of a Chapter in a late Book of Remarkable Providences, from the Calumnies of a Quaker at Pen-silvania.

Written By Cotton Mather, Minister of the Gospel.

And Recommended by the Ministers of Boston and Charleston

Printed at Boston in N. England by R. P. 1689. Sold by Joseph Brunning, at his Shop at the Corner of the Prison-Lane next the Exchange.

in his public behavior to be sure, but they also counted on Samuel Parris to provide them with an example of proper household worship . . . [and] a well-ordered family life."[29]

Parris dealt with his daughter's situation in the only way he knew, by praying with all his might, following the advice of Cotton Mather who wrote, "Prayer and Faith was the thing which drove the Divels from the Children."[30] Parris even called together pastors and respected men from the village to fast and pray with him. Nonetheless, the supplications to God did little to decrease the apparent suffering of the af-

Cotton Mather (pictured) urged Parris to pray fervently in order to exorcise the demons from his daughter.

flicted girls. In fact the hysteria seemed to deepen and take on new, even stranger symptoms such as muscle paralysis alternating with jerking body movements, hallucinations, and other torments.

Parris contacted William Griggs, a physician who was a friend of the family. Griggs proclaimed that Betty's problem was not natural but the work of Satan. Meanwhile, at the request of a neighbor, Mary Sibley, Tituba baked a "witch cake" made from flour mixed with the girls' urine. It was fed to the Sibley family dog in the belief this act of "white magic" would help break the witch's spell that was afflicting the children. When Parris found out, however, he beat Tituba severely, forcing her to confess to her role in the witch cake incident and demanding that she tell him about her knowledge of witchcraft.

Tituba believed that she was only trying to help alleviate the sufferings of Betty and Abigail, but to Parris her intent was demonic. As Breslaw writes: "In his mental world all occult powers were evil because they were derived from devilish associations. . . . Participation in magic was a form of blasphemy—it violated God's commandments—that could not be left unchallenged."[31] Tituba was further punished when, instead of receiving their gratitude, the girls named her as a witch along with two other women. After this shocking news, Parris sent Betty away to stay with his friend Stephen Sewall.

Meanwhile, when Tituba was examined by magistrates on March 1, 1692, she said that she had seen nine people—some of them from Salem—sign their names in the devil's book. This set off a wave of hysteria that spread to about a dozen other girls and women who also began to experience afflictions similar to those of Betty and Abigail. Soon accusations of witchcraft were flying about in a town already divided by decades of disagreement.

Fanning the Flames of Hysteria

The fact that the entire witchcraft matter blew up in Parris's home placed a great burden on the pastor, who only made matters worse. As Gragg writes: "The actions he took, and failed to take, proved to be crucial in creating an atmosphere of crisis, one in which a thoroughgoing witch hunt developed."[32]

Historians believe that if Parris had isolated the girls, the matter might have ended. Instead the pastor organized large town meetings where fasting and prayers were held to cure the afflicted. This gave the women and girls a public forum to display their lurid behavior. The afflicted were also allowed to attend church services, where they put on similar performances.

With Tituba in prison, the next woman to be accused of witchcraft was Martha Corey. On March 21 Parris took on the role of

During Martha Corey's trial, depicted in this woodcut, the afflicted girls writhed in agony and mimicked Corey's every movement.

court reporter, making a written record of Corey's interrogation by the magistrates. These proceedings were anything but normal, however, as Deodat Lawson described the scene in the courtroom:

> Mrs. Pope [one of the afflicted] complained of grievous torment in her Bowels as if they were torn out. She vehemently accused [Corey] as the instrument, and first threw her Muff at her; but that flying not home, she got off her Shoe and hit Goodwife [Corey] on the head with it. . . . The afflicted persons asked [Corey] why she did not go to the company of Witches which were before the meetinghouse mustering? Did she not hear the Drum beat? [33]

Meanwhile, during his Sunday sermons Parris continued to fan the flames of witch hysteria. In one sermon the pastor bellowed: "Christ knows how many Devils [are] among us, whither one or ten or 20," and "There are devils as well as saints . . . here in Christ's little Church." [34] Such accusations created an atmosphere of dread and panic, causing Lawson to write that the assembly "was struck with consternation, and they were afraid, that those that [sat] next to them, were under the influence of Witchcraft." [35]

44

Parris's sermons served to aggravate the state of affairs until a massive witch hunt broke out. There were more than twenty-five accusations made in April, about fifty in May, and by the end of the summer, so many that authorities could not keep track of them all. It is estimated that 140 to 200 people were either formally interrogated or arrested. Meanwhile, the finger-pointing spread to at least twenty-five other towns in Massachusetts. On May 27 Governor William Phips set up a special court of oyer and terminer to try all the witchcraft cases. During this time Parris acted as court reporter for fifteen cases and testified against ten of the accused. He is also believed to have been on panels that questioned the accused in court and in jail. During this time he was so busy that he stopped writing down his sermons in his sermon book.

The End of the Madness

When Parris did begin recording his sermons again, it was after more than a dozen people had been hanged. Yet the pastor still seemed to believe that the town was at war with the devil and that Satan had hatched a plot to destroy the Puritan foothold in the New World. Other authorities, however, seemed to be coming to their senses. By October Mather, Phips, and others began questioning the trials, the validity of the evidence, and the executions of seemingly innocent women and men.

Sensing that political winds had shifted, Parris suddenly softened the tone of his sermons. For example, on October 23, 1692, he spoke of the healing power of Christ's love. As Gragg explains:

> There is no mistaking the opportunistic element in Parris's sudden shift in tone; he clearly did not want to be an isolated advocate of more trials. Yet, it also represented an acknowledgement of an end to this particular crusade against the forces of evil. During the religious warfare, there had been numerous casualties. Neighbors had charged neighbors with heinous acts, the government had confiscated the property of the convicted and some of the accused, many had fled fearing prosecution, and almost two dozen people had lost their lives. In short, the lives of dozens of families had been shattered. It was, then, a time for healing and reconciliation. [36]

While Parris may have asked for reconciliation, his struggles continued in Salem. His full salary was not paid on time, his firewood was not provided, and other material issues continued to create an atmosphere of hostility between pro- and anti-Parris factions. Many who opposed the pastor were friends and relatives of those who had been convicted and executed as witches. Although Parris stayed on as Salem's pastor, he was continually challenged by a large group of dissenters who put great effort into forcing Parris's removal from the pulpit. They succeeded in late August 1697. After eight troubled years, Parris moved on, taking a job as pastor in the tiny village of Stow, Massachusetts.

In the following years, Parris married again (his wife Elizabeth died in 1696) and started a new family, having four children with Dorothy Noyes. He gave up preaching and worked at a variety of business endeavors in various towns throughout Massachusetts. Although he had a few successful ventures buying and selling real estate, Parris struggled financially throughout the rest of his life. He died in February 1720.

In the years since his death, critics have not been kind to the man at the center of the Salem witch hunts, although his beliefs were held by many during his lifetime. In the end, perhaps the words of Brook Adams written in 1887 in *The Emancipation of Massachusetts* best sum up the situation:

> Of Mr. Parris it is enough to say that he began the investigation with a frightful relish. . . . Mr. Parris behaved like a madman; not only did he preach inflammatory sermons, but he conducted the examinations, and his questions were such that the evidence was in truth nothing but what he put in the mouths of the witnesses; yet he seems to have been guilty of a darker crime, for there is reason to suppose he garbled the testimony it was his sacred duty to truly record. [37]

CHAPTER 3

Rebecca Nurse

Of the nineteen women and men hanged as witches in Salem, Rebecca Nurse was perhaps the most unlikely of victims. By all accounts, the seventy-year-old great-grandmother was a deeply religious woman who had spent her entire life studying the Bible. As Marion L. Starkey writes in *The Devil in Massachusetts: A Modern Enquiry into the Salem Witch Trials:* "Rebecca was, in the eyes of those who knew her well, the very essence of what a Puritan mother should be. Deeply pious, she was so steeped in Scripture that . . . when [she] spoke it was as if one of the grand old women of the Old Testament were speaking." [38] The fact that Rebecca Nurse ended her life swinging from a rope on Gallows Hill is a testament to the madness that gripped Salem in the spring of 1692.

Although the disgraceful treatment Nurse received at the end of her life is well documented, much less is known about her early years. Records show that Nurse was the daughter of William Towne and Joanna Blessing and that she was baptized in a Puritan church in Yarmouth, Norfolk, England, on February 21, 1621.

At some point after the baptism, the Townes left Yarmouth and moved to the New World. At that time people left England for a variety of reasons, including a desire to escape religious persecution, fear of a bubonic plague epidemic, and hardship because of an economic depression caused by falling wool prices. Whatever their reasons, the Townes were among the early settlers who took part in what was known as the "Great Migration" of English Puritans—approximately twenty thousand people who moved to Massachusetts between 1629 and 1643. Although it is unclear exactly when they arrived, it is known that they settled in Topsfield, Massachusetts, a tiny village about five miles north of Salem.

The character of the countryside in which Nurse spend her early years was described by Edward Johnson in 1640s as a "remote, rocky, barren, bushy, wild-woody wilderness, a receptacle for Lions, Wolves, Bears, Foxes, Rockoones . . . Bevers, Otters, and all kind of wild creatures, a place never afforded the Natives better than the flesh of a few wild creatures and parch't Indian corn incht out with Chesnuts and bitter Acorns." [39] As Rebecca Towne grew older, however,

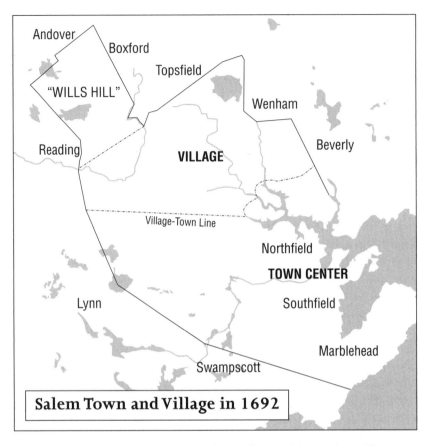

Salem Town and Village in 1692

New England became more settled and the "wild-woody wilderness" was slowly transformed into neat farms and modest wooden houses.

Topsfield was a typical New England village in which the Puritan church was at the center of all social activity. It is likely that the Townes were a traditional, deeply religious family. There is little doubt that Rebecca and her two sisters, Mary and Sarah, filled most of their free time in church or studying the Bible. Other times Rebecca would have spent her childhood as other Puritan girls did, cooking; cleaning; tending cows, pigs, and sheep; and helping her mother work a small vegetable garden.

Married to a Tray Maker

Rebecca Towne lived with her family until she was about twenty-three years old. In 1645 she married a local man, Francis Nurse (sometimes spelled Nourse). Nurse, born in England in 1618, was a relative newcomer to Massachusetts, having moved there in 1638. In the years following Rebecca's marriage, her sister Mary was wed to Isaac Esty, while sister Sarah married Peter Cloyse.

Rebecca's husband was a skilled woodworker. Although Francis Nurse was known as a "tray maker," he crafted many wooden items that were essential to the local farm families. These items included trays, butter churns, rakes, shovels, plows, washtubs, feed troughs for livestock, and small ten-gallon barrels called firkins. Nurse also worked as a "lot-layer" or surveyor for Salem. This work included laying out the boundaries for property and roads and arbitrating land border disputes between neighbors. In *Rebecca Nurse: Saint but Witch Victim,* Charles Sutherland Tapley gives a historian's view of Rebecca's husband:

> Francis Nurse was a man of clear judgement and a good mind. He was called upon repeatedly to administer justice and to arbitrate disputes. His untiring energy and persistence made him successful where less courageous characters would have failed. He was active and soldierly and by his ability contributed to the prosperity of Salem Village. Every man felt safe following his recommendations in any matter which he had carefully investigated.[40]

Francis's work provided the Nurses with enough money to purchase a nice farm at a place called Skerry's on a peninsula on the North River above Salem. In the years that followed, Rebecca Nurse had eight healthy children, four sons, and four daughters. With a large family, Nurse spent most of her life as a farmwife, preparing food, making and mending clothes, knitting, and spinning flax into yarn.

In 1676 Rebecca and Francis were well into middle age. After more than three decades at Skerry's, the Nurses were prosperous enough to buy a three-hundred-acre place known as the Townsend Bishops Farm, formerly owned by Massachusetts governor John Winthrop. Although this farm was the envy of many in the community, there was a dispute over the eastern boundary of the farm, which bordered land owned by the wealthy and powerful Putnams. This issue was never settled, and in the 1680s another bitter conflict arose when members of the Putnam family were accused of cutting timber on land belonging to the family of Mary Esty, Rebecca Nurse's sister. As Peter Charles Hoffer writes in *The Salem Witchcraft Trials: A Legal History:* "The dispute over timber . . . refused to die, for . . . animosities ran deep. Some of these must have spilled over into the way the Putnams regarded [all] the Topsfield women who lived in [Salem]—Rebecca Nurse, Mary Esty, and Sarah Cloyse."[41] This clash with the most influential family in Salem did not help the Nurses' standing in the community. The feud was exacerbated in 1688 when Samuel Parris, supported by the Putnams, first applied for the job as the Salem pastor.

Francis Nurse was on the church committee that interviewed Parris. Unlike previous pastors, Parris gave the committee a list of demands including a large salary, free firewood, and other expenses. The most rancorous confrontation arose over ownership of the parsonage and two acres surrounding it. Parris convinced some members of the committee to give him ownership of the house and land for free. His opponents, including Francis Nurse, said that the land could not be given away as it was deeded to the church for perpetual use by the pastor.

The land issue was never settled, but Nurse resigned from the church committee in disgust. He was supported in this move by his wife, who often counseled him on such matters. Although the Nurses

Rebecca Nurse's home still stands in Danvers, Massachusetts. Nurse, a devout seventy-year-old woman, was the most unlikely victim of the Salem witch trials.

had a strong dislike for Parris, he was made pastor of Salem's Puritan church in 1689. The antagonism did not abate, however, and many citizens of Salem, including the Nurses, refused to pay mandatory taxes for Parris's salary.

In October 1691 the dispute came to a head when the villagers selected five men, including Francis Nurse, to sit on a "rate committee" to negotiate Parris's salary. The committee voted to assess zero taxes to pay Parris. Members of the committee hoped that withholding his salary would force the pastor to resign. As a tough former businessman, however, Parris fought back, mustering support from Salem's most powerful citizens, including the Putnams whose land dispute with the Nurses continued. While the acrimony surrounding Parris remained unsettled, the divided town would have to confront a new, much more frightening problem that would engulf Rebecca Nurse, her sisters, and their families.

"Hellish Temptations"

The lines that were drawn over Parris hardened in early 1692 when the pastor's nine-year-old daughter, Betty, and her cousin, eleven-year-old Abigail, began behaving as if they were possessed by demons. The "afflicted girls" writhed and contorted their bodies and ran about the parsonage tipping over furniture and jumping from tables. During these hysterical episodes the girls accused several Salem women of witchcraft, including Parris's Indian slave Tituba. In early March, based on these allegations alone, the women were arrested. Two magistrates, John Hathorne and Jonathan Corwin held public inquiries into the matter. Afterward, the women were jailed in Boston awaiting trial for the crime of witchcraft, which carried the death penalty.

During the inquiry, Tituba hinted that there were many witches on the loose in Salem and a sort of delirium swept through the town. Neighbor began to fear neighbor, and before long at least eight other girls and women began exhibiting the hysterical symptoms of the afflicted girls. Two of them, twelve-year-old Ann Putnam Jr. and her mother, Ann Putnam Sr., would tragically implicate Rebecca Nurse as a witch.

On March 13 Ann Jr. said that she was haunted by the ghost of Goodwife Nurse. (Married women at this time were referred to as Goodwife, or Goody, instead of Mrs.) In the following days Ann Jr. claimed that Nurse "hath grievously afflicted by biting, pinching, and pricking me, [and] urging me to write in [the devil's] book."[42] Two days later Abigail Williams claimed that she also saw Nurse's ghost. On March 19 thirty-year-old Ann Sr. added validity to the young girls' claims by saying she too was visited by the specter of the

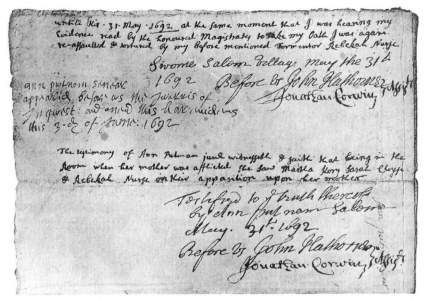

A transcript of the depositions of Ann Putnam and her daughter records their accusations of witchcraft against Rebecca Nurse.

old woman, saying: "[The] apparition of Rebecca Nurse did . . . set upon me in a most dreadful manner. . . . [She] appeared to me only in her shift, and brought a little red book in her hand, urging me vehemently to write in [the devil's] book; and because I would not yield to her hellish temptations, she threatened to tear my soul out of my body."[43] As word of the accusations spread through town several more afflicted girls added to the charges. Mary Walcott, about seventeen, stated that Nurse was responsible for killing five Salem citizens who had recently died. In addition, Walcott later testified she saw Nurse torment Ann Putnam Jr. and several other afflicted girls.

Vehement Suspicion of Witchcraft

The charges stunned Salem. While those previously accused of witchcraft were outcasts with few friends in Salem, Nurse was an unlikely witch. She was an elderly, gentle woman known for her piety and goodness. She and her husband were successful landowners who lived on a large farm surrounded by their children, grandchildren, and great-grandchildren.

Ironically, at the time Nurse's specter was allegedly flying about Salem tormenting and torturing the afflicted, the elderly matron was actually in bed, sick with a severe stomachache. And this was where Israel and Elizabeth Porter, two of Salem's most respected citizens, found her when they came to order her to appear at an inquisition before the magistrates. After she was apprised of the charges of witchcraft, Nurse could only answer weakly, "As to this thing I am innocent as a child unborn. . . . [What] sin has God found in me unrepented of that He could lay such an affliction on me in my old age?"[44]

When Nurse was brought to the meetinghouse on March 24, even the magistrates had a difficult time believing that the suspect could be a witch. In previous examinations, rather than behaving like an impartial judge, magistrate John Hathorne had acted more in the manner of a prosecuting attorney, bullying confessions out of the accused. This time Hathorne was unsure of himself and he even said to Nurse, "I pray God clear you if you be innocent, and if you be guilty discover you."[45]

Nurse pled innocent, telling Hathorne, "I am innocent and clear and have not been able to get out of doors these eight-nine days. . . . I never afflicted no child, no, never in my life."[46] Despite Nurse's words, moments after she uttered them one of the afflicted girls fell

In this Salem house, magistrate John Corwin conducted preliminary examinations of Rebecca Nurse and other people accused of witchcraft.

into convulsions, followed by another and another until the court-room erupted into chaos. According to Lawson the afflicted girls be-haved as if Nurse was:

> Biteing, Pinching, Bruising, Tormenting [them. Ann Putnam Sr.] had a grievous Fit, in the time of Examination, to the very great Impairing of her strength, and the wasting of her spirits, insomuch as she could hardly move hand, or foot, when she was carried out. Others were also grievously af-flicted, so that there were such an hideous scrietch (screech) and noise . . . as did amaze me.[47]

Afflicted girls fall into convulsions and point to an invisible flock of birds circling above a pair of suspected witches.

Moreover, the afflicted girls claimed that there were birds flying around Nurse. Whichever way she moved, the girls, acting together, mimicked her every move. The actions of the afflicted sealed Nurse's fate, as Starkey writes: "Watching the devil's choreography, the most impartial spectator could no longer credit Rebecca's plea of innocence. . . . Before the very eyes of the court, she was demonstrating her witchcraft." [48] Hathorne implored Nurse to confess, but she refused. Finally, like the other suspected witches, Nurse was carted off to Salem prison and locked in chains in a damp, cold, vermin-infested cell.

"Saints as Devils"

The Sunday following Nurse's examination, Reverend Parris preached that Satan would rather use a pious woman than a sinner for his evil deeds, telling his congregation "The Devil would represent the best saints as Devils if he could." [49] Although he did not mention Nurse by name, the implication was clear. Nurse's sister Sarah Cloyse could no longer bear the accusations. She got up from her pew and quickly exited the church. A strong March wind caused the door to slam hard behind her. Tapley writes: "Parris was determined that she should pay for this, and she was attended to in due season." [50] Within a week Cloyse was arrested and facing the same charges as her sister. Several weeks later Nurse's youngest sister, Mary Esty, was arrested for witchcraft after defending her sister. The message was clear—family members who came to the defense of the accused would also be arrested.

On June 2 Nurse was briefly removed from prison for a humiliating examination that would identify her as a witch. It was conducted by Sheriff George Corwin and several other men who were looking for physical marks allegedly made by the devil. For example, witches were said to have an extra nipple in order to suckle familiars, creatures such as black cats and birds that do the witch's bidding. The men were also looking for what were called devil's marks, insensitive spots of skin allegedly made by the devil's claws or teeth.

For this examination, Nurse was stripped, shaved from head to toe, then thoroughly examined for blemishes, moles, or scars that could be labeled diabolical. To find marks invisible to the eye, examiners would have prodded every inch of her body with a bodkin (a small, sharply pointed instrument for making holes in fabric or leather) until they found spots that did not bleed or feel pain. During Nurse's initial exam, the men thought they found a devil's mark on her genitals. Later, after a second examination, they decided it was only dry skin that was insensitive to the touch.

"The Courtroom Became a Madhouse"

A week after Nurse's mortifying exam, Bridget Bishop was the first accused witch to hang in Salem. On June 30 Nurse's case went to trial along with those of four other women. In court, John Putnam testified that Nurse's specter had murdered his eight-week-old child. Another woman, Nurse's neighbor Sarah Holton, claimed that the devilish ghost of Nurse had murdered her husband when he accidentally let his hogs into her garden. Holton told the court:

> Rebekah Nurs, who now stands charged for witchcraft, came to our house and fell a railing [started yelling at my husband], because our pigs got into her field. . . . And within a short time after this, my poor husband . . . was taken with a strange fit . . . being struck blind and struck down two or three times. . . . And all summer after, he continued in a languishing condition, being much pained in his stomach and often struck blind. But about a fortnight before he died he was taken with strange and violent fits, acting much like to our poor bewitched persons when we thought they would have died, And the doctor that was with him could not find what his distemper was. And the day before he died he was very cheerly, but about midnight he was again most violently seized upon with violent fits till the next night about midnight he departed this life by a cruel death. [51]

Although Holton's testimony was compelling, the judges ruled that "spectral evidence" was inadmissible in court. They stated that they could only convict Nurse on something "more considerable than the accused persons being represented by a specter unto the afflicted." [52]

While refusing to allow spectral evidence, the judges also considered a petition on behalf of Nurse from thirty-nine of Salem's most respected citizens. It read, in part: "[We] have known [Nurse] for many years and according to our observation . . . we never had any cause or grounds to suspect her of any such thing as she is now accused of." [53] Among the signers were several important and influential men who knew they were putting themselves in great danger by siding with an accused witch. In a dramatic turn of events, one of the signers was John Putnam who, after swearing out the original complaint against her, had now come to believe Nurse was innocent.

The petition and the inadmissibility of spectral evidence convinced the jury to return a verdict of not guilty. However, even as Nurse and her defenders breathed sighs of relief, the afflicted girls within the courtroom raised a hideous outcry. According to Starkey, "the courtroom became a madhouse. Out of the throats of the girls issued a howling and roaring that was . . . less than human. Their bodies jerked and snapped in the unearthly choreography of their convulsions." [54] The noise went beyond the courtroom and spread to the large crowd that was milling around the meetinghouse. Within seconds a cacophony erupted outside that drowned out the hysteria of the girls inside. These outbursts frightened the judges, who now believed the jury had made a dreadful mistake.

One of the judges stated that the verdict was not satisfactory. Another walked off the bench and threatened to have Nurse retried. Judge William Stoughton tried another ploy to reverse the verdict. The judge recalled an incident concerning Deliverance Hobbs, one of the several accused women who had actually confessed to the crime of witchcraft. Although historians believe Hobbs only did so in order to end her suffering in prison, she was also willing to implicate others, including Nurse. Stoughton recalled that when Hobbs was brought in to testify against Nurse, Nurse asked the judge, "What, do you bring [Hobbs]? She is one of us." [55] Nurse's words were interpreted by Stoughton to mean that Hobbs was a witch ("She is one of us"), and therefore an involuntary admission of guilt. The judge then asked: "Has the jury weighed the implication of this statement?" [56]

The jury went out again but could not agree on a verdict. They decided to ask Nurse what she meant when she said "She is one of us." In the tumult of the meetinghouse, Nurse did not hear the jury's question and so did not reply. The men on the jury then assumed that Nurse was admitting guilt. The jury changed the verdict to guilty and sentenced Nurse to hang.

The Hanging of Rebecca Nurse

After this, a zealous assistant minister, Nicholas Noyes, had Nurse excommunicated (expelled) from Salem church that very afternoon. She was brought in chains to the Salem meetinghouse to suffer further humiliation while the excommunication proceeded. To Nurse, who was a devout Puritan, excommunication meant certain damnation in hell.

In the days following her conviction, Nurse wrote a declaration to the court hoping to straighten out the matter concerning the jury's unanswered question about Hobbs. In the note, Nurse explained:

> [The] jury brought me in guilty upon my saying that Goodwife Hobbs and her daughter were of our company; but I intended no otherwise, then as they were prisoners with us, and therefore . . . do judge them not legal evidence against

their fellow-prisoners. And I being something hard of hearing and full of grief, none informing me how the Court took up my words, and therefore had no opportunity to declare what I intended, when I said they were of our company. [57]

Nurse believed it was natural to speak of Hobbs as "of our company" since they had been crowded together in jail. In addition, the letter made clear that Nurse was hard of hearing and so overwhelmed by anxiety that she had not heard the jury's questions.

The note was submitted to the court, while Nurse's sons traveled to Boston to submit a copy to Governor William Phips. Upon reading the note, Phips granted the old woman a reprieve from her death sentence. When they learned of the reprieve, however, the afflicted girls renewed their hysterical antics against Nurse. Several of them

Bridget Bishop, the first accused witch to be executed, is hanged on June 9, 1692. Three weeks later, Rebecca Nurse's case went to trial.

claimed they were dying. When Phips was apprised of this news, he recalled the reprieve.

Tuesday, July 19, 1692, was the second hanging day for witches in Salem and five accused women, including Rebecca Nurse, were scheduled to die. Observers noted that Nurse went to her death as she lived her life—as a good Christian with a forgiving heart, as Tapley writes: "Rebecca Nurse knew that that unseen land [heaven] to which she was going would be a better land than the one she had known; and she was confident that the light and the guidance of reason would be present there as it was not in the world she was leaving. Her mind was fixed upon higher scenes and filled with peace which the world could not take away." [58]

Given the facts that so many signed a petition in her favor and that she was first found not guilty, her death caused many in the crowd to question the process. As Nurse stood on the ladder to the gallows, she prayed to God to give some miraculous sign of her innocence. She also asked God to forgive those who had wronged her. There would be no miraculous intervention, however, and Rebecca Nurse was hanged.

After she was dead, Nurse's body was cut down and thrown into the crevices in the rocks on the side of the hill. No prayers were said, no respects given. For Nurse's relatives such an end must have been exceedingly painful. The night after the hangings young men of the Nurse family climbed up Gallows Hill under the cover of darkness and retrieved their grandmother's body. They brought it home and buried it, no doubt saying prayers in defiance of their church.

Clearing Her Name

Thirteen more were to hang for the crime of witchcraft, including Nurse's two sisters. In the following years, however, the Nurse family worked to exonerate Rebecca. They continued to quarrel with Parris for three years, sitting on committees that withheld his salary until he was forced to leave Salem. The new reverend, Joseph Green, a young man of only twenty-two, set about healing the town's wounds when he took over in 1697. He invited the Nurse family back to the church, but it was too late for Francis Nurse, who died that year. Green also worked to reverse the excommunication of Rebecca but it was not until 1712 that her excommunication was revoked.

Around this time Salem authorities were also anxious to put the matter behind them. In 1711 the government paid Nurse's survivors six hundred pounds for her wrongful death. In 1752, hoping to remove the taint of the witchcraft hysteria, Salem officials changed the

This memorial in Danvers, Massachusetts, commemorates the lives of Rebecca Nurse and the others executed for witchcraft.

name of the town to Danvers. The home where Rebecca and Francis Nurse spent the last years of their lives still stands there today, as a memorial park. In 1885 members of the Rebecca Nurse Memorial Society erected a monument on Nurse's grave. The inscription by John Greenleaf Whittier is perhaps the best way to remember the innocent woman accused of witchcraft by a town gone seemingly mad:

> O Christian Martyr who for Truth could die
> When all about thee owned the hideous lie!
> The world redeemed from Superstition's sway
> Is breathing freer for thy sake today.[59]

CHAPTER 4

Samuel Sewall

Samuel Sewall was one of the wealthiest men in Massachusetts and acted as a judge in the Salem witch trials. Although he sent nineteen men and women to their deaths, he was one of the few officials to later express regret. He was also a prolific writer who kept a detailed diary of his life. Although he did not write much about the witch trials, he did leave a valuable record that has been helpful to historians studying seventeenth- and eighteenth-century New England.

Samuel Sewall was born at Bishop Stoke, Hampshire, England, on March 28, 1652. When he was nine years old he moved with his family to Newbury, Massachusetts. Even at this young age Sewall was an observant boy with well-ordered thoughts, later noting that the day his family set sail, April 23, 1661, "was the Coronation of [King] Charles 2d. . . . [I clearly remember the] Thunder and Lightening of it." [60]

Sewall also remembered the long, dangerous voyage to Massachusetts, writing there was "nothing to see but Water and the Sky. . . . [I feared] I should never get to Shoar again." [61] Eight long weeks later, however, the ship bearing the Sewalls landed in Boston. A short boat ride to the north carried the family to Newbury, a town of less than fifty houses where sheep and cattle outnumbered the people.

A Lasting Education

As the son of a wealthy minister, Sewall was able to lead a life of privilege even in the primitive settlement of Newbury. His parents arranged for the pastor of the church, Thomas Parker, to prepare the boy for entry in Harvard when he turned fifteen. Sewall attended class with twelve other boys who were all planning on entering the ministry.

Unlike typically strict Puritan teachers of the day, Parker encouraged his students to think for themselves and record their thoughts in poems, as Ola Elizabeth Winslow writes in *Samuel Sewall of Boston*: "[Parker's] particular genius as a teacher would seem to have been his success in encouraging boys at this early age to go beyond the lessons of the day. He was particularly concerned also . . . that they make verses, in Latin and English, and some of them continued to do so throughout life, Samuel Sewall among them." [62] That

Sewall kept voluminous diaries throughout his life is perhaps testament to Parker's influence over the boy in those formative years.

Sewall was in school six days a week, and on Sundays he attended church all day, listening to sermons, singing psalms, and praying. Like the other boys in his class, Sewall was expected to take detailed, point-by-point notes during the sermon and recite them while standing before Parker on Monday morning. The boy must have enjoyed this exercise, as the habit of recording Sunday sermons in a notebook stayed with Sewall his entire life.

One of the wealthiest men in Massachusetts, Samuel Sewall acted as a judge in the Salem witch trials.

While the Puritans were strictly religious and very reserved in their lives, there were occasions when individual citizens seemed to go mad from the strain of living in such a rigid society. On one Sunday in 1663, for example, Sewall was sitting in church when a young woman, Lydia Wardell, walked into the meetinghouse naked. Wardell was sentenced to a whipping for her impertinence. As the entire town, including the eleven-year-old boy, watched, the young woman was tied to a fence post in front of the local tavern and given, according to Sewall's diary, "a certain twenty or thirty cruel stripes"[63] with the lash. Such typical punishment doled out in full public view must have influenced Sewall's outlook toward justice when he grew up and became a judge.

Studies at Harvard

Following the plan determined by his family, Sewall enrolled in Harvard in 1667 at the age of fifteen. The young man probably felt relieved that he had received such an excellent education as he was peppered with questions by the Reverend Mr. Charles Chauncy, president of Harvard. According to Sewall's diaries, he was asked: "[Could he] 'readily make, speake or write true Latin in prose?' [Had he] 'skill in making Verse?' [Was he] 'competently grounded in the Greeke Language so to be able to Construe and Grammatically to resolve ordinary Greeke, as in the Greeke Testament, Isocrates, and minor poets, or such like?'"[64] After satisfactorily answering the questions and passing several other tests, Sewall joined the other twenty-five young men who made up the Harvard student body at that time.

As a freshman, Harvard rules stipulated that Sewall speak in public eight times during the school year, attend public debates twice a week, leave town only with the college president's permission, and fraternize only with gentlemen of the best character. In addition, Harvard rules required students to avoid "rich and showy clothing . . . abstain from dice, cards, and every species of gaming for money . . . [and to cut their hair because] wearing of long haire in the manner of Russians and barbarous Indians, [is a practice] uncivil and unmanly whereby men do deforme themselves . . . and corrupt good manners."[65]

Harvard's schedule was even more rigorous than its student dress code. Like other students Sewall was up at sunrise for morning prayers and readings from the Old Testament. On a typical day, breakfast consisted of bread, butter, cheese, and beer. Classes lasted from 8:00 until 11:00 A.M. and after a two-hour lunch consisting of meat, bread, dried peas, hasty pudding, and apples, Sewall attended class until 5:00 P.M. At that time were evening prayers and readings

At the age of fifteen, Sewall enrolled at Harvard University, where he obtained a master's degree in divinity.

from the New Testament, and the day ended with supper at 7:30. All students were in their rooms by 9:00 P.M. and lights were put out at 11:00 P.M.

The curriculum Sewall studied, defined by college president Charles Chauncey, read:

> In the first yeare after admission for foure dayes of the weeke all Students shall bee exercised in the Study of the Greeke and Hebrew Tongues, onely beginning Logicke in the Morning towardes the latter end of the yeare unless the Tutor shall see Cause by reason of their ripenesse in the Languages to read Logicke sooner. Also they shall spend the second yeare in Logicke with the exercise of the former Languages, and the third year in principles of Ethickes and the fourth in metaphisiks and Mathematicks still carrying on their former studyes of the weeke for Rhetoricke, Oratory and Divinity. [66]

Marriage, Wealth, and Power

Sewall received his degree after four years at Harvard and decided to remain in school to get a master's degree in divinity. While working for his master of arts, Sewall wrote papers in Latin, Greek, and Hebrew that analyzed lofty questions from the Bible such as "Whether original sin be both sin and its punishment." [67]

Sewall was highly regarded by the faculty and was asked to speak at his commencement in 1674. In attendance was Hannah Hull, who was very impressed with Sewall's discussion of original sin. According to Sewall, Hull "set her affection"[68] upon him that day. As fate would have it, Hannah's father, John, was one of the wealthiest men in Massachusetts. John Hull started his career as a silversmith and took the job as mintmaster of the colony in 1652. This enviable position involved minting 5 million shilling coins from pinewood (metal was scarce at that time). From this work, Hull was paid one shilling per twenty produced. By the 1670s Hull had parlayed his fortune into an import/export company with a fleet of ships that controlled a large percentage of the colony's trade.

Sewall and Hannah Hull were married in 1676 in the Old South Church in Boston, an institution founded by John Hull. After the marriage Sewall joined the church but apparently abandoned thoughts of joining the ministry. Instead he went to work for his father-in-law in Boston buying and selling goods such as fish, rum, rope, hats, drinking glasses, and other products.

A woodcut depicts Boston's Old South Church where Samuel Sewall and Hannah Hull were married in 1676.

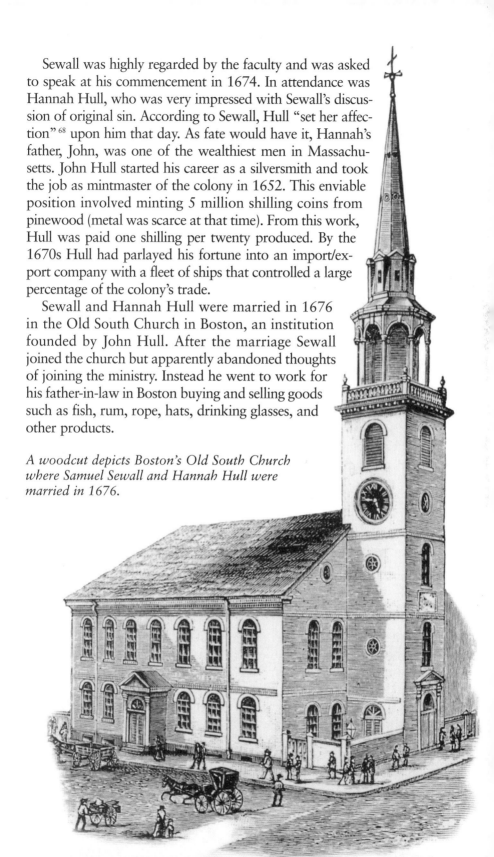

Although he had wealth and power, like all the other Puritans in the New World Sewall was not immune from the deadly diseases that periodically swept through the colony. In a diary entry marked "Fall 1678," Sewall dryly records, "I was seized with the Small Pocks and brought very near to death; so near that I was reported to be dead. But it pleased GOD and his Mercy to Recover me." [69] Two months later Sewall suffered a relapse that achieved only brief mention in his journal.

The year after his recovery Sewall decided to go into public service by joining the "freemen." This elite group of about a thousand—in a population of twenty-five thousand—acted as jurors, selectmen, surveyors, and more. Sewall was made one of eight constables in Boston. This job put him in charge of Boston's "night watch," overseeing watchmen who "duley examine all Night walkers after ten of the clock at night . . . to inquire whither they are going, and what their business is . . . to see all noises in the streets stilled, and lights put out." [70] Those who were deemed suspicious were arrested and taken before a magistrate in the morning. Although the night watch was not a popular job among freemen, Sewall enjoyed the work so much he kept at it for thirty more years. He seemed to enjoy strolling the streets of Boston late at night, often noting in his diary lunar eclipses, snow depth, temperature, and other observations.

After serving as constable for two years, Sewall took on an additional position. In 1681 he was appointed by the general court to take over the Massachusetts printing press. By controlling one of the only presses in North America, Sewall was able to make his influence known, printing books and articles about subjects that interested him. Sewall combined religious books with scientific studies about Halley's comet, which appeared that year. He also published sermons with titles such as "The High Esteem in Which God Hath the Death of the Saints."

"Do All the Good That's in Your Power"

Sewall's career in publishing came to an end when John Hull died on October 1, 1683. With the death of Hull, Sewall and his wife and four children inherited a fortune. Hull's property alone made Sewall the largest landholder in Boston and allowed him to collect rents on warehouses, shops, stables, and private residences. In a colony where money was short, the rents were often paid in firewood, pigs, chickens, fish, butter, hay, turkey, cattle, cheese, corn meal, homemade clothing, and anything else that could be produced by local farmers and artisans. At the age of thirty-one, Sewall had prestige, respect, and riches beyond the dreams of most.

Sewall's easy wealth, however, did not seem to interfere with his religious beliefs, which remained the guiding force in his life. Toward this end, Sewall generously shared his wealth with institutions that educated and inspired. In a poem entitled "Lines for a Sun Dial," Sewall eloquently stated his philosophy:

Keep in God's way; keep pace with evry hour

Hurt none; do all the Good that's in your Power.

Hours can't look back at all; they'll stay for none

Tread sure, keep up with them, and All's your own. [71]

To do the good within his power, Sewall donated many acres of land to worthy causes. He gave one thousand acres of land to Harvard College, eleven acres to the town of Sherborn, Massachusetts, for a parsonage, and one acre for a meetinghouse in Kings Town, Rhode Island. He also made cash donations to help churches hire ministers or improve their facilities. Sewall's generosity was analyzed by T.B. Strandness in *Samuel Sewall: A Puritan Portrait:* "As to his motives, they were doubtless influenced by the thought that in the right use of one's possessions lay promise of divine reward. On the other hand, he was a kindly man, sufficiently guileless to do good simply because he thought God wished it." [72]

"The Most Horrible Witchcraft"

Philanthropy was only one role that Sewall doubtlessly believed God had chosen for him. Another was the use of his intelligence and power to guide the governmental affairs of the colony. Sewall was granted that chance in 1684, when he was appointed to the magisterial seat in the court of assistants formerly held by his father-in-law. This body was run by a small faction of men who made up the entire judicial, executive, and legislative branches of Massachusetts government.

The court had jurisdiction over all laws in the colony including those banning rape, murder, piracy, theft, and so on. As a magistrate on this court, Sewall was exposed to the underbelly of Puritan society while doling out harsh sentences. For example, a man named John Balston broke into a widow's house and stole some of her property. For this crime Balston was to be "branded with the letter B on the forehead [for burglar] and have his Right eare Cutt [off]." [73] Sewall was little bothered by such severe punishments. For example, in one diary entry made after a murderer was hanged, Sewall wrote dryly that the man was "turned off about 1/2 an hour past five. The day was very comfortable." [74]

Sewall saw a weekly parade of petty criminals and murderers but he never acted as a judge in any cases concerning witchcraft. Although the colony's English rulers had made witchcraft a capital crime in 1641, the law received little attention until February 1692 when accusations of witchcraft first surfaced in Salem. Within the next several months the isolated incidents erupted into a serious crisis. William Phips, the new governor of Massachusetts, described the problem in a letter to the royal authorities:

> I found the Province miserably harrassed with the most Horrible witchcraft or Possesssion of Devills which had broke in

Massachusetts governor William Phips took the charges of witchcraft in Salem very seriously and appointed an emergency court to try the accused.

upon several Townes, some scores of poor people were taken with preternaturall torments some scalded with brimstone some had pins stuck in their flesh others hurried into the fire and water and some dragged out of their houses and carried over the tops of trees and hills for many Miles together. . . . And there were many committed to prison upon suspicion of Witchcraft before my arrivall. The loud cries and clamours of the friends of the afflicted people . . . and many others prevailed with mee to . . . [discover whether] witchcraft might be at the bottom or whether it were not a possession. [75]

"Belief in the Reality of Witches"

Phips did not mention that those "taken with preternaturall torments" were ten girls and women, most of them under the age of seventeen. Their accusations had already ensnared forty-two people who had been examined before magistrates and jailed, awaiting trial. Since the local courts were in peril of being overwhelmed by these witchcraft cases, Phips appointed an emergency court of judges on May 27 to hold trials for the accused. It was an ad hoc court (one formed for the one specific purpose) called a court of oyer and terminer. In England, courts of oyer and terminer were set up for cases of social disorder on the scale of riots and revolutions.

Phips appointed members of his governing council to the court of oyer and terminer. All were experienced magistrates who were instructed to reach final verdicts in their cases. No appeals would be granted. The new deputy governor, William Stoughton, was made chief justice of the court. Sewall's eight years on the bench presumably attracted the attention of Phips, and the forty-year-old judge was also asked to serve on the court. He was joined by Wait Winthrop, Peter Sargent, and John Richards, all from Boston, and Bartholomew Gedney and Jonathan Corwin of Salem. According to Chadwick Hansen, author of *Witchcraft of Salem,* "No more experienced or distinguished a court could have been assembled anywhere in English America." [76] While the justices may have been distinguished, their superstitions were deeply ingrained, according to author Ola Elizabeth Winslow:

Samuel Sewall [and his fellow judges] brought to the trial session an almost unchallenged heritage of belief in the reality of witches as the devil's agents. To seventeenth century men and women . . . witches were the willing agents of Satan, pledging to overthrow God's kingdom on earth. Their presence in any community was a *sign* the [leaders] ignored at their peril. . . . To deny the reality of these evil agents in 1692 would have meant to question also a literal heaven and hell, all angels, all devils, fire brimstone . . . and even Judgement Day itself.[77]

By the time the court of oyer and terminer met in Salem on June 2, 1692, witch hysteria had swept through Salem and the surrounding towns. Neighbors were accusing neighbors and children allegedly afflicted with witches' torments were convincing authorities to lock up formerly respectable citizens. More than a hundred suspects were suffering under inhumane conditions in jail.

"'Twas Awfull to See"

For Sewall, a dedicated diarist who recorded trivia such as the phases of the moon, there is an incongruous lack of details about what he thought of the witch panic. For example, one of the few times he mentioned the situation was before he was appointed to the court. On April 11 Sewall traveled to Salem to watch the examination of two accused witches, Sarah Cloyse and Elizabeth Proctor. As the women were harshly questioned by local magistrates, the afflicted girls fell into fits, shrieking and screaming that the accused were sticking pins in their flesh. Sewall, however, recorded few details of these curious events, writing only: "[The] persons accused of Witchcraft were examined; was a very great Assembly; 'twas awful to see how the afflicted persons were agitated. Mr. Noyes pray'd at the beginning, Mr. Higginson concluded."[78]

After Sewall's court was convened, it condemned all who were accused of witchcraft. During this entire period there were little more than half a dozen entries into Sewall's diaries concerning the witch trials. The comments that were made were very brief. They gave no information as to the judge's true feelings while the court pronounced death sentences on each and every one of the accused.

One of the condemned, Reverend George Burroughs, was a friend of Sewall's. The two men met when students at Harvard. In the years following graduation the two dined together on occasion, and Burroughs gave a sermon at Sewall's church at least once. Burroughs was Salem's minister from about 1680 to 1683 but left in a bitter dispute over his salary, leaving many enemies behind in the small town. In mid-March 1692 Sewall, who was a banker, even lent Burroughs twenty-six pounds in Boston. Six weeks later, however, Burroughs was accused of witchcraft. According to the minister of Boston's Old North Church, Cotton Mather, in *Wonders of the Invisible World*, Burroughs was

Executioners prepare Reverend George Burroughs for hanging. Judge Sewall condemned Burroughs, an old friend of his, to death for witchcraft.

Accused by five or six of the Bewitched as the Author of their Miseries; he was Accused by eight of the Confessing Witches, as being an Head Actor at some of their Hellish Randezvouzes, and one who had the promise of being a King in Satans Kingdom. . . . [He] was accused by nine persons for extraordinary Lifting, and such Feats of Strength, as could not be done without a Diabolical Assistance.[79]

It is unclear why so many Salem citizens made such outlandish claims against a man who was once their pastor, but Burroughs's

August 4 trial was typical of the other witch trials. When he looked at the afflicted girls who were his accusers, they fell into screaming fits. (Their suffering was so extreme that the judges ordered them removed from the courthouse for their own safety.) A local woman gave testimony claiming that a ghost had told her that Burroughs had murdered his two deceased wives. And a local man claimed that Burroughs exhibited superhuman strength by carrying a full barrel of molasses using only his fingers. Judge Sewall apparently saw nothing unusual in this seemingly ridiculous testimony. The judge's diary entry from this time mentions that there was a terrible earthquake in Jamaica. There is no mention, however, of the trial nor of his longtime friend whom he had just sentenced to death.

When Burroughs and four others were executed on August 19, Sewall did mention a few details of a hanging, one of the few times he did so, writing:

> This day . . . George Burroughs, John Willard, Jn. Procter, Martha Carrier and George Jacobs were executed at Salem, a very great number of Spectators being present. Mr. Cotton Mather was there. . . . All of them said they were innocent, Carrier and all. Mr. Mather says they all died by a Righteous Sentence. Mr. Burroughs by his Speech, Prayer, protestation of his Innocence, did much move unthinking persons.[80]

If Sewall felt any grief over the harsh treatment of his old acquaintance it is not apparent in his diary. In fact, he omitted many details of the dramatic events surrounding Burroughs's death. For example, the condemned reverend stood on the gallows and recited the Lord's Prayer. According to witness Robert Calef, the prayer was "so well worded, and uttered with such composedness, and such . . . fervency of Spirit, as was very affecting, and drew Tears from many (so that it seemed . . . that the Spectators would hinder the Execution)."[81] Although such a recitation was thought impossible by a wizard, local authorities insisted Burroughs be executed before protests could be organized.

"Press'd to Death"

Sewall continued to perform his duties, apparently without hesitation, on the court of oyer and terminer. The court met again, on September 9 and 17, and condemned fifteen more to hang. (Not all were executed, however, as some confessed to witchcraft, an act that allowed them to escape execution.)

On September 19 one of the most gruesome executions took place when eighty-year-old Giles Corey, accused of wizardry, refused to speak or answer the questions of Sewall and the other judges. Corey was taken to an open field near the courthouse, stripped naked, and made to lie on the ground while tons of rocks were piled on his chest. He finally died after several hours. Sewall reported Corey's death in his typical sparse manner: "About noon, at Salem, Giles Corey was press'd to death for standing mute."[82]

Corey's gruesome execution seemed to have had an unsettling effect upon the populace, and the witch hysteria began to wind down. Although eight more were hanged on September 22, on October 8 Governor Phips banned the use of spectral testimony, that is, statements

Judge Sewall pronounces Giles Corey guilty of witchcraft and orders him pressed to death beneath several tons of rock.

by the afflicted that were allegedly revealed to them by ghosts. Since most cases were based on such evidence, no more trials were held.

On October 29, 1692, Phips prohibited further arrests, released many accused witches, and dissolved the court of oyer and terminer. In December Phips appointed Sewall to the superior court, which heard and quickly dismissed more than fifty witchcraft cases, prompting Mather to write: "They cleared the accused as fast as they tried them . . . and the land had peace restored unto it."[83]

Sewall remained a judge on the superior court for another twenty-five years and became the chief justice in 1717, a job he held until 1728, two years before his death.

Take the Blame and Shame

History will never know the exact thoughts of Sewall during the Salem witch trials or why the judge kept no records of the proceedings. In

In 1697 Sewall expressed regret for his role in the Salem witchcraft proceedings, and his apology was read publicly.

Samuel Sewall and the World He Lived In, N.H. Chamberlain speculates as to why Sewall did not write in his diary at the time: "He evidently was ashamed, cast down, full of sorrow, and probably afraid of personal prosecution and loss of property at the hands of the survivors suing for damages. The court he belonged to was no doubt illegal, and its proceedings, as judged by the ethics of English law, more than questionable." [84]

The trials must have troubled Sewall, however, as he alone was the only judge to ever express public regret over the proceedings. The inspiration to confess came about on January 14, 1697, when the general court ordered a day of fasting and soul-searching to reflect on the tragedy in Salem. By this time Sewall had suffered his own tragedies, losing several of his infant children to disease. In an act of humility and contrition, Sewall drafted a letter of apology, which was read by his pastor Samuel Willard at his meetinghouse on the day of fasting:

> Samuel Sewall, sensible of the reiterated strokes of God upon himself and family; and being sensible, that as to the Guilt contracted, upon the opening of the late Commission of Oyer and Terminer at Salem (to which the order for this Day relates) he is, upon many accounts, more concerned than any that he knows of, Desires to take the Blame and Shame of it, Asking pardon of Men, And especially desiring prayers that God, who has an Unlimited Authority, would pardon that Sin and all other his Sins; personal and Relative: And according to his infinite Benignity, and Sovereignty, Not Visit the Sin of him, or of any other, upon himself or any of his, nor upon the Land. [85]

After the apology was read, Sewall stood up and bowed his head, having written the last word on the Salem witchcraft trials by those who were participants in the events.

Arguing Against Slavery

Sewall's role in the Salem witch trials was not the only controversy that marked the judge's life. In 1700 Sewall wrote a three-page tract called "The Selling of Joseph" that used religious theories to argue against slavery, which was legal in the colonies. Sewall printed up hundreds of copies and gave them away for the rest of his life.

While working for justice for slaves, Sewall lived the rest of his days as a wealthy merchant and respected judge. When he was seventy-seven years old he decided to assemble all his writings into *The Diary of Samuel Sewall,* which covers nearly fifty-six years of his life from December 1673 to October 1729, three months before his death. Since it was first published in 1878, this day-to-day record of life in Massachusetts in the seventeenth and eighteenth centuries has been considered a precious gift by historians. Although much of the information is trivial, taken together it provides a detailed picture of life in America's colonial years. When Sewall died on January 1, 1730, he left behind a record for the ages. While his entries during the witch trials were few, his apology for the miscarriage of justice remains a tribute to a man who seemed to value religion over wealth and justice above all.

CHAPTER 5

Cotton Mather

Cotton Mather was an influential Puritan minister at Boston's Old North Church and one of the most prolific writers of his day. One of his 382 books, *Wonders of the Invisible World,* provides details of the Salem witch trials. In this book Mather leaves little doubt that he believes witches are not figments of the imagination but are as real as the trees in the forest and the fish in the sea.

It is not surprising that Cotton Mather was a respected religious authority in seventeenth-century Massachusetts. His father, uncles, and grandfathers held tremendous influence over the shape and direction of Puritanism in New England for three generations. Mather's grandfather, John Cotton, was a pastor in England but believed that clergy should have less power. He was forced to leave and moved to Boston in 1635, where he became head of that town's Congregational Church.

Mather's other grandfather, Richard Mather, was a pastor in England but was expelled from the Church of England in 1635 for criticizing Anglican worship ceremonies. He moved to the Massachusetts Bay Colony, where he was immediately recognized as a leader of the Puritan church in Dorchester, outside of Boston. He held that position for thirty-three years.

Mather's father, Increase, was a minister of Boston's Second Congregational Church where he shaped the lives and values of second-generation New England Puritans through his authorship of 130 books and pamphlets. Increase Mather served as president of Harvard from 1685 to 1701. When Increase married Richard Cotton's daughter Maria, they cemented a powerful religious bond between Boston's most powerful clans. When their first child, Cotton Mather, was born on February 12, 1663, he carried the names of the two families.

Increase had little doubt that Cotton would someday be a powerful religious leader in Massachusetts, chosen for this role by God: "If ever [a] Father had a particular Faith for a child, then I had so for that child, of whom I could with Assurance say, God has blessed him, yea, and He shall be blessed." [86]

"Rebuked My Play-Mates"

While Increase may have felt that his son was chosen by God, Cotton was also blessed with a family that valued education. Six of his closest male relatives were Harvard graduates and eight of them were ministers. Cotton's house was filled with books written by his relatives and the sounds of psalms and prayers recited by family members. On Sundays the boy would sit in church listening with rapt attention to his father's sermons. During the week his home was a center for religious and political discussions attended by ministers, educators, and government officials.

Increase Mather (pictured) believed that his son Cotton would become a powerful religious leader in Massachusetts.

From the earliest moments of his life Cotton absorbed the intellectual banter that surrounded him. He learned to pray as soon as he learned to speak, inventing prayers rather than reciting standard litanies. By the time he was four he could read and write. On Sunday evenings he would return home after listening to his father preach and write out the sermons from memory. At the age of seven the boy read Scripture during most of his waking hours away from school, sometimes covering fifteen chapters a day.

Not surprisingly, young Cotton was a morally upright child who tried to shape and mold the behavior of his friends. He wrote that he "Obliged them to *Pray*. [And] Rebuked my Play-mates, for their Wicked *Words* and *Ways*." [87] This righteousness came with a price, however, as his friends did not always appreciate the lessons of the preacher's precocious son. As Mather writes, "Sometimes I suffered from them, the persecution of not only *Scoffs* . . . but *Blows* also, for my *Rebukes*." [88]

A Child at Harvard

Despite the reaction of his playmates, Mather continued to excel at his studies. In 1675 the eleven-and-a-half-year-old became the youngest student ever accepted to Harvard in the college's forty-year history. (Increase Mather had been twelve when he was first accepted to Harvard.) Although not yet a teenager, Mather was able to pass Harvard's strict entrance exam that required him to read and speak Hebrew and understand the classics of Virgil, Ovid, and Homer in their original Latin and Greek. The boy could also speak and write Latin so well that he could translate sermons from English to Latin even as they were spoken by the preacher.

Mather's prospects were tempered somewhat because he had developed a stammer. This was an unfortunate development. Mather was believed by many to have been chosen by God to someday lead the Puritan church, which required him to give two long sermons every Sunday and to speak at many meetings during the week. The boy's stuttering caused great consternation within the Mather family. The boy wrote that it was "a Thing as much despaired of, as anything in the World." [89] To solve the problem, a few months into the boy's freshman year at Harvard Mather and his parents spent an entire day fasting and praying for an end to his stammering.

While his stutter did not go away immediately, Mather worked extremely hard to learn to speak slowly and deliberately. Eventually he overcame the stammer, but he feared for many years that it would return, writing, "By careful deliberation, my public services were freed from any blemish [of the stammer], yet I was . . . kept in continual *care* and *fear* and *faith* concerning it." [90]

Mather graduated from Harvard in 1678 when he was only fifteen years old, the age of the typical freshman students of that time. Mather, however, was no typical student. At the commencement ceremony Uriah Oakes, the president of Harvard, recalled Mather's grandfathers while expressing the feelings of many respected citizens gathered that June day:

> Mather is named Cotton Mather. What a name! My hearers, I mistake; I ought to have said what names! . . . [Should] he resemble his venerable grandfathers, John Cotton and Richard Mather, in piety, learning, splendor of intellect, solidity of judgement, prudence, and wisdom, he will indeed bear the palm [be successful]. And I have confidence that in this young man Cotton and Mather will be united and flourish again. [91]

A Young Preacher

After graduation Mather took on the role of teacher for a few years, conducting classes for five of his eight brothers and sisters along with a few neighborhood students. In 1680 he followed his destiny to the pulpit and began preaching Sunday sermons. His first was on August 22 at the Dorchester church founded by his grandfather John Cotton, the second was in North Church where Increase Mather was pastor. Soon he preached at the First Church where Richard Mather was once pastor. Although he had an offer to lead a church in New Haven, Connecticut, Mather decided to work as an assistant to his father, joining him in the ministry at North Church in 1681. Two years later Increase was named president of Harvard, but the elder Mather performed this duty by traveling to Cambridge on occasion, while maintaining his position at the North Church.

Although he was conducting religious services, Cotton Mather continued with his studies, earning a master's degree at Harvard when he was nineteen. Mather also began keeping a detailed diary around this time, and the pages indicate that the young man thought of little else but God, the Bible, and his own perception of himself as an imperfect sinner. For example, neatly numbered passages from a May 3, 1683, entry reveal a day in the life of Mather:

> 1. I began the day with expressing before the Lord my belief of his being a rewarder of those who diligently seek him. . . .
>
> 2. I then read the chapters of the Bible which occurred to me . . . [and] turned those chapters into prayers for the Lord.

Puritan clergyman John Cotton was Cotton Mather's grandfather. In 1686 Mather and his wife moved into John Cotton's old home.

3. Afterwards I essayed in meditation, to affect my own heart with a sense of the manifold vileness wherewith I have provoked God; my *old sins* and my *late sins*. . . .

4. This done, I sang unto the Lord that hymn . . . called Confessions of Sin.

5. Hereupon I spent some time in pondering . . . some occasional reflections.

6. I then went again into my supplications, wherein I considered that after all my vileness, the Lord is willing to deal with me in the covenant of grace.[92]

The rest of the day was spent in similar manner, with Mather singing hymns and psalms, praying, attending a church meeting where he preached a sermon, visiting and praying with a sick neighbor, and finally praying for salvation before going to sleep.

Marriage and Sorrow

By the time he was twenty-two, Mather was preaching up to five sermons a week, sometimes within the course of two or three days. The young man, however, remained a bachelor. Having resisted temptation to sin, Mather began to fear that he might no longer be able to defend against his sexual urges. In typical fashion, the pastor set aside November 7, 1685, as a day for prayer on the subject of marriage. According to biographer Abijah P. Marvin, Mather prayed that if God would have him "embrace a celibacy, he would evermore take contentment in it [but] since his inclinations and invitations did now seem to recommend a married state, he begged that God would lead him in the way wherein he should go." [93]

In January 1686 Mather must have believed his prayers answered when he met the beautiful fifteen-year-old Abigail Phillips, daughter of the respected Captain John Phillips. Mather was smitten by the young woman and wasted no time proposing. In May, with Abigail one month shy of her sixteenth birthday, the couple were married. They set up house in John Cotton's old home, where Mather was born. Tragedy struck in January 1688, however, when the couple's firstborn daughter, also named Abigail, died at the age of five months.

Despite his pronounced grief, Mather delivered on the afternoon of his daughter's death a sermon entitled "Right Thoughts in Sad Hours, Representing the Comforts and the Duties of Good Men Under All Their Afflictions; and Particularly . . . the Untimely Death of Children." In the sermon, he offered his flock "such considerations as I would this day quiet my own tempestuous and rebellious heart with . . . [though the] dying of a Child is like the tearing of a limb from us." [94]

"The Enchantment of the Children"

The death of baby Abigail was the first of a series of crises that Mather would face in 1688. In March, due to political criticism of the colony's English rulers, a warrant was issued for Increase Mather on charges of defamation. Increase managed to elude the law by hiding for several days and then escaping aboard a ship to England where he hoped to straighten out the matter. In his father's absence, Cotton was appointed pastor of the North Church, where he preached to as many as fifteen hundred people every Sunday. Then, in midsummer a fearful case of witchcraft broke out that would have long-lasting repercussions for Massachusetts—and for Mather.

In July 1688 the children of a "sober and pious"[95] mason, John Goodwin, began having strange fits. In the book *Memorable Provinces* that Mather would write about the event, the pastor describes the scene:

> Sometimes [the children] would be Deaf, sometimes Dumb, and sometimes Blind, and often all at once. One while their

A Puritan minister in Boston preaches from his pulpit. As pastor of Boston's North Church, Cotton Mather preached to as many as fifteen hundred people each Sunday.

Tongues would be drawn down their Throats; another while they would be pull'd out upon their Chins, to a prodigious length. They would have their Mouths opened unto such a Wideness, that their Jaws went out of joint; and anon they would clap together again with a Force like that of a strong Spring-Lock. The same would happen to their Shoulder-Blades, and their Elbows, and Hand-Wrists, and several of their joints. . . . They would make the most piteous out-cries, that they were cut with Knives, and struck with Blows that they could not bear. . . . Yea and their Heads would be twisted almost round. [96]

Mather had experience with victims of witchcraft well before the Salem witch trials. Here, Mather prays over a possessed young woman.

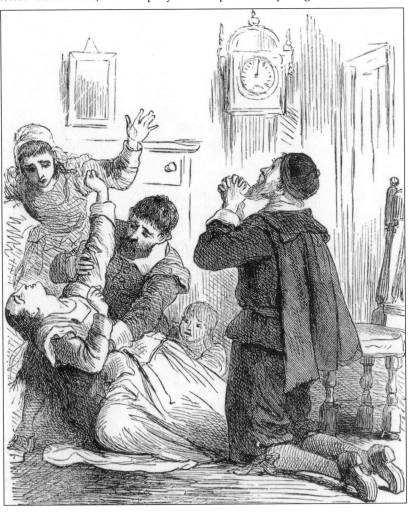

Doctors and preachers were called in and it was determined that the fits started after one of the children quarreled about some missing linens with an Irish washerwoman named Goodwife Glover. This old woman was Roman Catholic, a religion that was much hated by the Puritans, and John Goodwin implied that she was the cause of his children's misery.

Glover was arrested and questioned by magistrates. Although she spoke only the native Irish language known as Gaelic, according to Mather, "the Hag had not the power to deny her interest in the Enchantment of the Children; and when she was asked, Whether she believed there was a God? Her Answer was too blasphemous and horrible for any Pen of mine to mention." [97] Glover was asked to recite the Lord's Prayer, a task Puritans believed was impossible for a witch to perform. Again the language barrier prevented Glover from responding properly to the request. She was arrested and Mather, along with four other ministers, held a day of prayer at the Goodwin house, after which the torments of the girls temporarily ceased.

While Glover was in jail, another odd incident helped seal her fate. A six-year-old Boston boy claimed that one night he saw, according to Mather, a "Black thing with a Blue Cap in the Room, Tormenting him; and he complained most bitterly of a Hand put into the Bed, to pull out his Bowels." [98] The boy's mother went to the prison and accused Glover, asking why she had done this awful deed. Glover allegedly replied that it was revenge for what was being done to her. Hearing this story, Mather confronted Glover, who did not deny her guilt. In addition, she claimed that she had been in a witches' meeting with four others. Mather then offered to pray for Glover, but the old woman said she could pray for herself. Mather writes, "However, against her will I pray'd with her, which if it were a Fault it was in excess of Pitty." [99]

"Seven Times Hotter than It Was"

On the way to her execution, Glover warned Mather that her death would not relieve the torments of the children because there were other witches living in Boston. Although she gave Mather their names, the preacher never revealed them. After Glover was hanged on November 16, 1688, her statement as to their continued agony proved to be true. As Mather writes:

[The] Three children continued in their Furnace as before, and it grew rather Seven times hotter than it was. . . . The Fits of the Children yet more arriv'd unto such Motions as were beyond the Efficacy of any natural Distemper in the World. They would bark at one another like Dogs and again purr like so many Cats. They would sometimes complain that they were in a Red-hot Oven, sweating and panting. . . . They would cry out of dismal Blowes with great Cudgels laid upon them. . . . And one of them would be roasted on an invisible Spit, run into his Mouth, and out at his Foot, he lying, and rolling, and groaning. . . . Sometimes also he would have his head so forcibly, tho not visibly, nail'd unto the Floor.[100]

In modern times, such behavior might warrant an appointment with a psychiatrist. In the seventeenth century, however, it was seen as proof of witchcraft and the devil. Mather would no more have questioned this than he would have doubted the existence of angels, heaven, or even God. In fact, on November 20 Mather took thirteen-year-old Martha Goodwin into his home for two purposes. One was to cure her of her afflictions, the second was to observe and record her behavior in order to conclusively confirm the existence of witchcraft and refute those who denied its reality.

During this time Goodwin's frightening fits of madness and hysteria continued until Mather and four other ministers were able to conduct an exorcism that was supposed to drive Satan from the girl's body. Goodwin was still struck with fits two times a week for many months, but by spring she was cured. She finally moved from Mather's home in June 1689.

Witchcraft Moves to Salem

Mather recorded his experiences with Glover and the Goodwins in *Memorable Provinces,* which became an instant best seller. The book was widely read and discussed among seventeenth-century Puritans and was one of the few books found in the meager library of Samuel Parris, pastor of the Puritan church in Salem, a small village about fifteen miles from Boston. Parris turned to *Memorable Provinces* for guidance in early 1692, when his nine-year-old daughter Betty and her eleven-year-old cousin Abigail began exhibiting hysterical fits similar to those experienced by Martha Goodwin.

It is unclear when Mather first became aware of the Salem witch panic, but there is little doubt that when three women were arrested on charges of felony witchcraft in late February 1692, the news quickly spread to Boston. One of the accused witches, a South American Indian woman named Tituba, was Parris's slave. When she was questioned by magistrates, she implied that there were dozens of witches living in and around the small village.

After Tituba and the other women were locked in prison awaiting trial, Parris followed Mather's advice in *Memorable Provinces.* The reverend isolated his daughter and niece and attempted to cure them with fasting and prayer. This only seemed to make matters worse, however. Charges and countercharges began flying about Salem and soon dozens of people—some of them the town's most respected citizens—were arrested for witchcraft. Meanwhile, the number of afflicted girls grew to more than ten.

By this time Mather had traveled to Salem in order to assess the situation. Sensing an emergency, he offered to take six of the afflicted girls into his home in order to cure them. This might have stopped the witch hunt immediately, as David Levin writes in *Cotton Mather:* "Mather's behavior in the Goodwin case suggests that he would have tried to avoid publicizing the names [that the afflicted girls] cried out. . . . Mather's plan might have limited the girls' powerful effect on one another." [101]

Although Mather's offer was rejected by the Salem authorities, the preacher took it upon himself to confront the Salem witch problem, writing in *Wonders of the Invisible World:* "[At] this extraordinary Time of the *Devils coming down in great Wrath upon us,* there are too many Tongues and Hearts thereby *set on fire of Hell.* . . . I have indeed set my self to Countermine the whole Plot of the Devil against New-England . . . as far as . . . [I] can comprehend such a Work of Darkness." [102]

Warnings Ignored

There is little doubt that Mather used his considerable knowledge and influence to advise Governor William Phips in May 1692, as the Salem and Boston jails filled with dozens of people accused of witchcraft. On May 27 Phips set up the court of oyer and terminer specifically to hear the charges against these prisoners. Mather no doubt helped pick the judges, as three of the seven on the court were his friends—and members of his church.

Although he was ill and could not travel to Salem, Mather continued to play an active role in the trials even before the court held its first hearings on May 31. Mather wrote to one of the judges, John Richards, and warned him not to take too seriously "spectral testimony" or statements by the afflicted that were allegedly revealed to them by ghosts or apparitions:

> I must . . . beg you that . . . you do not lay more stress upon pure specter testimony than it will bear. . . . It is very certain that the devils have sometimes represented the shapes of persons not only innocent but very virtuous. . . . Moreover, I do suspect that persons who have too much indulged themselves

An afflicted girl falls to the floor during trial proceedings. Mather was convinced that the girls' hysteria was proof that the devil intended to destroy Massachusetts.

in malignant, envious, malicious, ebullitions [violent outpouring of emotion] of their souls may unhappily expose themselves to judgment of being represented by devils, of whom they never had any vision, and with whom they have much less written a covenant.[103]

Mather advised the judge to rely only on confessions, and then only those that were credible, not those offered under great duress and fear. The reverend ended the letter suggesting that some of the accused be spared execution and given a lesser penalty.

Despite Mather's warnings, the judges allowed spectral testimony. Throughout the summer of 1692 several dozen men and women were found guilty of witchcraft and sentenced to death.

Vigorously Endorsing Executions

Although Mather was too sick to attend any of the trials, he was present at the August 19 execution of former Salem minister George Burroughs and four others. As Burroughs was mounting the steps of the gallows, he eloquently expressed his innocence to the crowd who began to have doubts about the execution. After he was hanged a violent backlash threatened to erupt among the townsfolk. According to witness Robert Calef, Mather acted quickly to quell a revolt against the authorities: "[As] soon as [Burroughs] was turned off, Mr. Cotton Mather, being mounted upon a Horse, addressed himself to the people, partly to . . . possess the People of [Burroughs's] guilt; saying that the Devil has often been transformed into an Angel of Light; and this did somewhat appease the People, and the Executions went on."[104] This act, ensuring that four more accused were hanged, changed Mather's perceived role from one of a cautious reverend to that of an advocate for execution. In the following five weeks, nine more were convicted and executed for witchcraft in Salem.

After the execution of George Burroughs, Cotton Mather (pictured) acted quickly to stave off a revolt among the villagers.

Although he attended none of the trials, Mather was thoroughly informed by those who did. In letters he wrote about the subject, he indicated that the continued hysteria exhibited by the afflicted girls at the trials proved to him that witches and the Devil were out to destroy Massachusetts. By this time Mather seemed to be ignoring his

In late 1692, Cotton Mather began to write Wonders of the Invisible World, *a book in which he claims the witch trials were necessary to help rid the world of evil.*

The Wonders of the Invisible World:

Being an Account of the

T R Y A L S

O F

Several Witches,

Lately Excuted in

NEW-ENGLAND:

And of feveral remarkable.Curiofities therein Occurring.

Together with,

I. Obfervations upon the Nature, the Number, and the Operations of the Devils.

II. A fhort Narrative of a late outrage committed by a knot of Witches in *Swede-Land*, very much refembling, and fo far explaining, that under which *New-England* has laboured.

III. Some Councels directing a due Improvement of the Terrible things lately done by the unufual and amazing Range of *Evil-Spirits* in *New-England*.

IV. A brief Difcourfe upon thofe *Temptations* which are the more ordinary Devices of Satan.

By COTTON MATHER.

Publifhed by the Special Command of his EXCELLENCY the Governeur of the Province of the *Maffachufetts-Bay* in *New-England.*

Printed firft, at *Bofton* in *New-England*; and Reprinted at *London*, for *John Dunton*, at the *Raven* in the *Poultry*. 1693.

---

own previous warnings about spectral evidence. As Levin writes: "[All his] wisdom, skepticism, and respect for human liberties did not prevent Mather . . . from acquiescing in some of the executions and vigorously endorsing others."[105]

In early September, even before the last accused witches were hanged, Mather began to write *Wonders of the Invisible World*. Besides describing the afflictions, accusations, trials, and executions, Mather uses the book to justify the entire episode to "vindicate the country, as well as the judges and juries,"[106] also stating in summary that by "the *Goodness* of God we are once more out of the present danger of this *Hobgoblin Monster*."[107]

On October 3 Increase Mather used his influence to denounce the use of spectral evidence. Less than a week later Governor Phips prohibited the court from using this type of evidence in witchcraft trials. By the end of the month the governor banned further arrests, released the accused witches from jail, and dissolved the court of oyer and terminer. The Salem witch delusion was over.

A Man of Learning and Science

Mather will long be remembered as a stern religious leader and an advocate of witch executions. The Salem witch panic was only a short chapter in an otherwise illustrious career, however. Mather was a voracious reader who could write in eight languages including Iroquois. Throughout his life he wrote and published hundreds of books, most of them religious and historical tracts including the eight-hundred-page *Magnalia Christi Americana (The Mighty Deeds of Christ in America)*, the most detailed account of early American history from that era.

Later in life Mather became involved with a group of scientists in the Royal Society of London. These men were interested in the natural history of North America, and Mather often wrote long detailed letters to the society describing muskrats, moose, wild turkeys, and other animals not found in England. Mather also studied and wrote about eclipses, weather, magnetism, earthquakes, and other phenomena of nature.

Cotton Mather died of fever one day after his sixty-fifth birthday on February 13, 1728. Although he is remembered for his role in the witch hysteria in Salem, his last statement before he died more accurately reflects his life—"Remember only that one word, *Fructuosus*"[108] ("fruitful" in Latin). For a man who lived to preach, write, study, and help the afflicted, it is an appropriate epitaph for one of the most brilliant men of his times—or of any other.

NOTES

Introduction: Hanging the Witches

1. Quoted in Frances Hill, *A Delusion of Satan*. New York: Doubleday, 1995, p. 11.

Chapter 1: Tituba

2. Charles W. Upham, *Salem Witchcraft*, vol. 2. Williamstown, MA: Corner House, 1971, p. 2.

3. Elaine G. Breslaw, *Tituba: Reluctant Witch of Salem*. New York: New York University Press, 1996, p. 15.

4. Upham, *Salem Witchcraft*, p. 2.

5. Breslaw, *Tituba*, p. 20.

6. Quoted in Kenneth Silverman, *The Life and Times of Cotton Mather*. New York: Harper & Row, 1984, pp. 238–39.

7. Breslaw, *Tituba*, p. 99.

8. Quoted in Chadwick Hansen, *Witchcraft at Salem*. New York: George Braziller, 1969, p. 33.

9. Quoted in Upham, *Salem Witchcraft*, p. 95.

10. Quoted in George Lincoln Burr, ed., *Narratives of the Witchcraft Cases 1648–1706*. New York: Barnes & Noble, 1975, pp. 153–54.

11. Quoted in Burr, *Narratives of the Witchcraft Cases 1648–1706*, p. 413.

12. Quoted in Hansen, *Witchcraft at Salem*, p. 2.

13. Quoted in Upham, *Salem Witchcraft*, pp. 23–24.

14. Quoted in Upham, *Salem Witchcraft*, p. 25.

Chapter 2: Samuel Parris

15. Larry Gragg, *A Quest for Security*. New York: Greenwood, 1990, p. xv.

16. Paul Boyer and Stephen Nissenbaum, *Salem Possessed: The Social Origins of Witchcraft*. Cambridge, MA: Harvard University Press, 1974, p. 154.

17. Gragg, *A Quest for Security*, p. 12.

18. Quoted in Gragg, *A Quest for Security*, p. 13.

19. Gragg, *A Quest for Security*, p. 32.

20. Peter Charles Hoffer, *The Devil's Disciples*. Baltimore: Johns Hopkins University Press, 1996, p. 21.

21. Boyer and Nissenbaum, *Salem Possessed*, p. 156.

22. Hoffer, *The Devil's Disciples*, p. 29.

23. Breslaw, *Tituba*, p. 79.

24. Gragg, *A Quest for Security*, p. 50.

25. Samuel Parris, *The Sermon Notebook of Samuel Parris, 1689–1694*, Eds. James F. Cooper Jr. and Kenneth P. Minkema. Boston: Colonial Society of Massachusetts, 1993, p. 93.

26. Parris, *The Sermon Notebook of Samuel Parris, 1689–1694*, pp. 50–51.

27. Parris, *The Sermon Notebook of Samuel Parris, 1689–1694*, p. 22.

28. Quoted in Hansen, *Witchcraft at Salem*, p. 55.

29. Gragg, *A Quest for Security*, p. 70.

30. Cotton Mather, *Memorable Providences, Relating to Witchcrafts and Possessions*. Ann Arbor, MI: University Microfilms, 1977, p. 126.

31. Breslaw, *Tituba*, p. 109, 111.

32. Gragg, *A Quest for Security*, p. 116.

33. Quoted in Roger Thompson, *The Witches of Salem: A Documentary Narrative*. London: Folio Society, 1982, p. 53.

34. Parris, *The Sermon Notebook of Samuel Parris, 1689–1694*, pp. 148–49.

35. Quoted in Gragg, *A Quest for Security*, p. 121.

36. Gragg, *A Quest for Security*, p. 146.

37. Brook Adams, *The Emancipation of Massachusetts*. Boston: Houghton Mifflin, 1962, pp. 394–95.

Chapter 3: Rebecca Nurse

38. Marion L. Starkey, *The Devil in Massachusetts: A Modern Enquiry into the Salem Witch Trials*. New York: Time, 1963, p. 66.

39. Quoted in David Grayson Allen, "Vacuum Domicilium: The Social and Cultural Landscape of Seventeenth Century New England," American Centuries . . . View from New England, www.americancenturies.mass.edu/classroom/curriculum_12th/unit1/lesson2/allen.html.

40. Charles Sutherland Tapley, *Rebecca Nurse: Saint but Witch Victim*. Boston: Marshall Jones, 1930. pp. 5–6.

41. Peter Charles Hoffer, *The Salem Witchcraft Trials: A Legal History*. Lawrence: University of Kansas Press, 1997, p. 27.

42. Quoted in Paul Boyer and Stephen Nissenbaum, eds., *Salem-Village Witchcraft*. Boston: Northeastern University Press, 1993, p. 18.

43. Quoted in Boyer and Nissenbaum, *Salem-Village Witchcraft*, p. 19.

44. Quoted in Starkey, *The Devil in Massachusetts*, p. 70.

45. Quoted in Hansen, *Witchcraft at Salem*, p. 51.

46. Quoted in Starkey, *The Devil in Massachusetts*, p. 72.

47. Quoted in Burr, *Narratives of the Witchcraft Cases 1648–1706*, p. 159.

48. Starkey, *The Devil in Massachusetts*, p. 73.

49. Parris, *The Sermon Notebook of Samuel Parris, 1689–1694*, p. 151.

50. Tapley, *Rebecca Nurse*, p. 58.

51. Quoted in Thompson, *The Witches of Salem*, p. 119.

52. Quoted in Starkey, *The Devil in Massachusetts*, p. 162.

53. Quoted in Boyer and Nissenbaum, *Salem-Village Witchcraft*, p. 34.

54. Starkey, *The Devil in Massachusetts*, p. 163.

55. Quoted in Burr, *Narratives of the Witchcraft Cases 1648–1706*, p. 358.

56. Quoted in Starkey, *The Devil in Massachusetts*, p. 164.

57. Quoted in Upham, *Salem Witchcraft*, p. 285.

58. Tapley, *Rebecca Nurse*, p. 67.

59. Quoted in Benjamin Ray, "Rebecca Nurse Homestead," Etext, 2002. http://etext.virginia.edu/salem/witchcraft/Homestead.html.

Chapter 4: Samuel Sewall

60. Quoted in Ola Elizabeth Winslow, *Samuel Sewall of Boston*. New York: Macmillan, 1964, p. 5.

61. Quoted in Winslow, *Samuel Sewall of Boston*, p. 6.

62. Winslow, *Samuel Sewall of Boston*, p. 22.

63. Samuel Sewall, *The Diary of Samuel Sewall, 1674–1729*, vol. 3, ed. M. Halsey Thomas, New York: Farrar, Strauss, and Giroux, 1973, p. 48.

64. Quoted in Winslow, *Samuel Sewall of Boston*, p. 31.

65. Quoted in Samuel Elliot Morison, *Harvard College in the Seventeenth Century*. Cambridge: Harvard University Press, 1936, p. 81.

66. Quoted in Morison, *Harvard College in the Seventeenth Century*, pp. 144–45.

67. Quoted in T.B. Strandness, *Samuel Sewall: A Puritan Portrait*. East Lansing: Michigan State University Press, 1967, p. 21.

68. Sewall, *The Diary of Samuel Sewall, 1674–1729*, vol. 3, p. 149.

69. Sewall, *The Diary of Samuel Sewall, 1674–1729*, vol. 1, p. 46.

70. Quoted in Strandness, *Samuel Sewall*, p. 62.

71. Quoted in Strandness, *Samuel Sewall*, pp. 51–52.

72. Strandness, *Samuel Sewall*, p. 55.

73. Quoted in Strandness, *Samuel Sewall*, p. 64.

74. Quoted in Strandness, *Samuel Sewall*, p. 64.

75. Quoted in Burr, *Narratives of the Witchcraft Cases 1648–1706*, p. 196.

76. Quoted in Hansen, *Witchcraft at Salem*, p. 122.

77. Winslow, *Samuel Sewall of Boston*, pp. 113–14.

78. Sewall, *The Diary of Samuel Sewall, 1674–1729*, vol. 1, p. 289.

79. Cotton Mather, *Wonders of the Invisible World*. London: John Russell Smith, 1862, pp. 120–21.

80. Sewall, *The Diary of Samuel Sewall, 1674–1729*, vol. 1, p. 294.

81. Quoted in Burr, *Narratives of the Witchcraft Cases 1648–1706*, pp. 360–61.

82. Sewall, *The Diary of Samuel Sewall, 1674–1729*, vol 1, p. 295.

83. Quoted in Strandness, *Samuel Sewall*, p. 74.

84. N.H. Chamberlain, *Samuel Sewall and the World He Lived In*. New York: Russell & Russell, 1967, p. 168.

85. Sewall, *The Diary of Samuel Sewall, 1674–1729*, vol 1, p. 367.

Chapter 5: Cotton Mather

86. Quoted in Silverman, *The Life and Times of Cotton Mather*, p. 7.

87. Quoted in Silverman, *The Life and Times of Cotton Mather*, p. 14.

88. Quoted in Silverman, *The Life and Times of Cotton Mather*, p. 14.

89. Quoted in Silverman, *The Life and Times of Cotton Mather*, p. 15.

90. Quoted in Abijah P. Marvin, *The Life and Times of Cotton Mather, D.D., F.R.S.* New York: Haskell House, 1973, p. 16.

91. Quoted in Marvin, *The Life and Times of Cotton Mather, D.D., F.R.S*, p. 8.

92. Quoted in Marvin, *The Life and Times of Cotton Mather, D.D., F.R.S*, p. 34.

93. Quoted in Marvin, *The Life and Times of Cotton Mather, D.D., F.R.S*, p. 63.

94. Quoted in Silverman, *The Life and Times of Cotton Mather*, p. 76.

95. Quoted in Burr, *Narratives of the Witchcraft Cases 1648–1706*, p. 99.

96. Quoted in Burr, *Narratives of the Witchcraft Cases 1648–1706*, pp. 101–102.

97. Quoted in Burr, *Narratives of the Witchcraft Cases 1648–1706*, p. 103.

98. Quoted in Burr, *Narratives of the Witchcraft Cases 1648–1706*, p. 105.

99. Quoted in Burr, *Narratives of the Witchcracft Cases 1648–1706*, p. 106.

100. Quoted in Burr, *Narratives of the Witchcraft Cases 1648–1706*, pp. 107–108.

101. David Levin, *Cotton Mather.* Cambridge, MA: Harvard University Press, 1978, p. 197.

102. Mather, *Wonders of the Invisible World*, pp. 3–4.

103. Quoted in Alice Dickinson, *The Salem Witchcraft Delusion.* New York: Franklin Watt, 1974, p. 158.

104. Quoted in Burr, *Narratives of the Witchcraft Cases 1648–1706*, p. 361.

105. Levin, *Cotton Mather*, p. 200.

106. Quoted in Levin, *Cotton Mather*, p. 218.

107. Mather, *Wonders of the Invisible World,* p. 217.

108. Quoted in Silverman, *The Life and Times of Cotton Mather*, p. 422.

FOR FURTHER READING

Books

Marc Aronson, *Witch-Hunt: Mysteries of the Salem Witch Trials.* New York: Atheneum Books for Young Readers, 2003. The story of two Salem families and their roles in the witch hysteria.

Norma Jean Lutz, *Cotton Mather: Author, Clergyman, and Scholar.* Philadelphia: Chelsea House, 2000. A biography of the man whose writings about the devil and witchcraft were central to the prosecution during the Salem witchcraft trials.

Jenny MacBain, *The Salem Witch Trials: A Primary Source History of the Witchcraft Trials in Salem, Massachusetts.* New York: Rosen Central Primary Source, 2003. Original documents concerning the outbreak of the hysteria, the examinations, the trials, and the executions of the victims.

Laura Marvel, ed., *The Salem Witch Trials.* San Diego: Greenhaven, 2003. Presents theories concerning the seventeenth-century witch trials, and offers possible explanations for the behavior of those accused.

WORKS CONSULTED

Books

Brook Adams, *The Emancipation of Massachusetts*. Boston: Houghton Mifflin, 1962. A reading of the early history of Massachusetts that is highly critical of Puritan culture and tradition and laudatory of the revolutionary period.

Paul Boyer and Stephen Nissenbaum, *Salem Possessed: The Social Origins of Witchcraft*. Cambridge, MA: Harvard University Press, 1974. An analysis of the events in Salem focusing on personal conflicts between rival families.

———, eds., *Salem-Village Witchcraft*. Boston: Northeastern University Press, 1993. Source documents from the seventeenth-century witch panic including dispositions, trial notes, letters of mercy, land deeds, wills, and other official papers.

Elaine G. Breslaw, *Tituba: Reluctant Witch of Salem*. New York: New York University Press, 1996. A biography of the Indian slave who was at the center of the Salem witchcraft controversy.

George Lincoln Burr, ed., *Narratives of the Witchcraft Cases 1648–1706*. New York: Barnes & Noble, 1975. This book, first published in 1914, contains some of the original court transcripts of the Salem witch trials along with letters and essays written by Cotton and Increase Mather and others.

N.H. Chamberlain, *Samuel Sewall and the World He Lived In*. New York: Russell & Russell, 1967. First published in 1897, this biography of a judge in the Salem witch trials helps put the subject's actions in perspective with the tenor of the times.

Alice Dickinson, *The Salem Witchcraft Delusion*. New York: Franklin Watt, 1974. A book written about Salem, the witch trials, and various participants in the tragedy.

Larry Gragg, *A Quest for Security*. New York: Greenwood, 1990. A biography of Samuel Parris, the pastor of Salem Church during the witch hysteria.

Chadwick Hansen, *Witchcraft at Salem*. New York: George Braziller, 1969. A thorough reading of the Salem witch hysteria by an author who believes witchcraft was actually practiced in Salem and some of those hung were not innocent.

Frances Hill, *A Delusion of Satan*. New York: Doubleday, 1995. One of the newest books written about the Salem madness by an English author who uses modern psychology and feminism to question the forces behind the witch hunts.

Frances Hill, *The Salem Witch Trials Reader.* Cambridge, MA: Da Capo, 2000. Source documents, many of them from the seventeenth century, that relate to the accusers, the accused, the myths surrounding, and reality of the Salem witch incident.

Peter Charles Hoffer, *The Devil's Disciples.* Baltimore: Johns Hopkins University Press, 1996. An examination of the Salem witch incidents with a focus on the personalities involved.

———, *The Salem Witchcraft Trials: A Legal History.* Lawrence: University of Kansas Press, 1997. The New England witch episodes studied from a legalistic standpoint.

Carol F. Karlsen, *The Devil in the Shape of a Woman.* New York: W.W. Norton, 1987. A study of female gender roles as they pertained to the Salem witch panic and how the sexual structuring of Puritan society led innocent women to the gallows.

David Levin, *Cotton Mather.* Cambridge, MA: Harvard University Press, 1978. A biography of the influential Boston minister covering the first forty years of his life.

Abijah P. Marvin, *The Life and Times of Cotton Mather, D.D., F.R.S.* New York: Haskell House, 1973. A scholarly biography that relies on many extended source quotes to describe the life of a man who dedicated his life to religion and writing.

Cotton Mather, *Memorable Providences, Relating to Witchcrafts and Possessions.* Ann Arbor, MI: University Microfilms, 1977. One Mather's earliest written works, this treatise on witchcraft was used by judges as a guidebook in order to convict people of the felony of witchcraft in Salem two years after its publication.

———, *Wonders of the Invisible World.* London: John Russell Smith, 1862. A true historical record of the trials of several witches in Salem written by a prominent Massachusetts pastor, demonologist, and prolific author.

Samuel Elliot Morison, *Harvard College in the Seventeenth Century.* Cambridge: Harvard University Press, 1936. The history of the famous Massachusetts college from its founding in 1650 through the early 1700s.

Samuel Parris, *The Sermon Notebook of Samuel Parris, 1689–1694.* Eds. James F. Cooper Jr. and Kenneth P. Minkema. Boston: Colonial Society of Massachusetts, 1993. Complete and partial texts of the fifty-two surviving sermons preached by the controversial pastor at the center of the Salem witch trials.

Samuel Sewall, *The Diary of Samuel Sewall, 1674–1729.* Vols. 1–3. Ed. M. Halsey Thomas. New York: Farrar, Strauss, and Giroux, 1973. The prolific writings of the man who was a judge on the court of oyer and terminer. Describes daily life and his observations from the witch trials.

Kenneth Silverman, *The Life and Times of Cotton Mather.* New York: Harper & Row, 1984. A biography of one of the most famous Puritan ministers, examined in the context of life in seventeenth-century Boston.

T.B. Strandness, *Samuel Sewall: A Puritan Portrait.* East Lansing: Michigan State University Press, 1967. A biography of the man who rose to prominence in Massachusetts and who sat as a judge during the witch trials in Salem.

Marion L. Starkey, *The Devil in Massachusetts: A Modern Enquiry into the Salem Witch Trials.* New York: Time, 1963. First published in 1949, this work examines the witchcraft incidents through the lens of post–World War II America when anti-Communist hysteria was sweeping across the country.

Charles Sutherland Tapley, *Rebecca Nurse: Saint but Witch Victim.* Boston: Marshall Jones, 1930. A brief biography of one the most unlikely victims of the witch hysteria with a detailed recounting of her trial and execution.

Roger Thompson, *The Witches of Salem: A Documentary Narrative.* London: Folio Society, 1982. The story of the Salem witch incident as told through the words of various authors from the seventeenth century to modern times.

Charles W. Upham, *Salem Witchcraft.* Vols. 1 and 2. Williamstown, MA: Corner House Publishing, 1971. First published in 1867, this two-volume set contains more than nine hundred pages that study the Salem witch trials. The first volume is a detailed history of Salem Village; the second covers the accusations, examinations, trials, and executions in vivid detail.

Ola Elizabeth Winslow, *Samuel Sewall of Boston.* New York: Macmillan, 1964. A biography of a prominent player in the witch trials based largely on the prolific writings and diaries of the subject himself.

George Malcolm Yool, *1692 Witch Hunt: The Layman's Guide to the Salem Witchcraft Trials.* Bowie, MD: Heritage, 1992. Depositions, written courtroom testimony, and legal documents from the witch trials updated to modern English.

Internet Sources

David Grayson Allen, "Vacuum Domicilium: The Social and Cultural Landscape of Seventeenth Century New England," American Centuries . . . View from New England, www.americancenturies.mass. edu/classroom/curriculum_12th/unit1/lesson2/allen.html. A site that explores New England history with a collection of artifacts and documents.

Douglas Linder, "Salem Witchcraft Trials 1692," Famous Trials, June 2002. www.law.umkc.edu/faculty/projects/ftrials/salem/SALEM.HTM. A comprehensive study of the Salem witch hysteria with biographies of the accused, arrest and death warrants, examinations and evidence, letters from the accusers, and dozens of other interesting articles.

Benjamin Ray, "Rebecca Nurse Homestead," Etext, 2002. http://etext. virginia.edu/salem/witchcraft/Homestead.html. The Web site of the museum established in the still existing home of one of Salem's most respected residents who was nonetheless hung as a witch.

PICTURE CREDITS

ABOUT THE AUTHOR

Stuart A. Kallen is the author of more than 170 nonfiction books for children and young adults. He has written on topics ranging from the theory of relativity to the history of rock and roll. In addition, Mr. Kallen has written award-winning children's videos and television scripts. In his spare time Stuart A. Kallen is a singer/songwriter/ guitarist in San Diego, California.